Student Workbook

Show What You Know® on the OAA

3

Preparation for the Ohio Achievement Assessment

Name: _____

Published by:
Show What You Know® Publishing
A Division of Englefield & Associates, Inc.
P.O. Box 341348
Columbus, OH 43234-1348
Phone: 614-764-1211
www.showwhatyouknowpublishing.com
www.passtheoaa.com

Copyright © 2010 by Englefield & Associates, Inc.

Ohio's state assessment Item Distribution was obtained from the Ohio Department of Education Web site.

All rights reserved. No part of this book, including interior design, cover design, and icons, may be reproduced or transmitted in any form, by any means (electronic, photocopying, recording, or otherwise).

Printed in the United States of America
11   20 19 18 17 16 15 14 13 12 11 10 9 8 7 6 5 4

ISBN: 1-59230-412-5

Limit of Liability/Disclaimer of Warranty: The authors and publishers have used their best efforts in preparing this book. Englefield & Associates, Inc., and the authors make no representations or warranties with respect to the contents of this book and specifically disclaim any implied warranties and shall in no event be liable for any loss of any kind including but not limited to special, incidental, consequential, or other damages.

Acknowledgements
Show What You Know® Publishing acknowledges the following for their efforts in making this assessment material available for Ohio students, parents, and teachers.

Cindi Englefield, President/Publisher
Eloise Boehm-Sasala, Vice President/Managing Editor
Jill Borish, Production Editor
Jennifer Harney, Editor/Illustrator

About the Contributors
The content of this book was written BY teachers FOR teachers and students and was designed specifically for Ohio's state assessment for Grade 3 Reading and Mathematics. Contributions to the Reading and Mathematics chapters of this book were also made by the educational publishing staff at Show What You Know® Publishing. Dr. Jolie S. Brams, a clinical child and family psychologist, is the contributing author of the *Worry Less About Tests* and *Test-Taking Hints for Test Heroes* chapters of this book. Without the contributions of these people, this book would not be possible.

Table of Contents

Introduction v

Worry Less About Tests 1

Test-Taking Hints for Test Heroes 11

Reading 25
   Introduction 25
   Questions I Will Answer on Ohio's State Assessment 26
   Item Distribution for Ohio's State Assessment for Grade 3
      Reading Assessment 28
   Scoring 29
   Glossary of Reading Terms 33
   Directions for Practice Test 1 39
   Practice Test 1 40
   Directions for Practice Test 2 67
   Practice Test 2 68

Mathematics 99
   Introduction 99
   Questions I Will Answer on Ohio's State Assessment 100
   Item Distribution for Ohio's State Assessment for Grade 3
      Mathematics Assessment 104
   Scoring 104
   Glossary of Mathematics Terms 108
   Glossary of Mathematics Illustrations 116
   Directions for Practice Test 1 121
   Practice Test 1 122
   Directions for Practice Test 2 155
   Practice Test 2 156

Introduction

The purpose of Ohio's state assessment is to measure student learning. Throughout the school year, students are exposed to a wide variety of concepts from a range of disciplines, only some of which are tested by the assessment. Yet it is important that all Ohio Academic Content Standards be taught in order to ensure that students have a well-rounded understanding of the third-grade curriculum. Students who have been taught the elements of the Ohio Academic Content Standards curriculum will have been exposed to all that is assessed by Ohio's state assessment. Nonetheless, students will benefit from the review of key details as they prepare to take this assessment.

This *Student Workbook* is designed to help students better understand the types of information they will see on Ohio's state assessment. This book will help students review important elements assessed by Ohio's state assessment; it is not a substitute for continuous teaching and learning, which take place both in and outside the classroom. But, as with any assessment, it is a good idea to review principles that have been taught and learned prior to taking Ohio's state assessment.

Introduction

This *Student Workbook* includes many features that will benefit students as they prepare for Ohio's state assessment.

The first two chapters, Worry Less About Tests and Test-Taking Hints for Test Heroes, were written especially for third graders. Worry Less About Tests offers advice on how to reduce anxious feelings about tests, and Test-Taking Hints for Test Heroes gives strategies students can use to do their best on tests.

The Reading and Mathematics chapters of this book will introduce students to the types of questions they will answer on Ohio's state assessment. In addition, there are two practice tests for each subject. These tests will help students become familiar with the look and feel of Ohio's state assessment. Each practice test is a great opportunity for students to practice their test-taking skills.

For easy reference, this Student Workbook correlates with the *Teacher Guide* (sold separately).

Worry Less About Tests

Introduction

Many of us get nervous or anxious before taking a test. We want to do our best, and we worry that we might fail. You may have heard of Ohio's state assessment, although you may not be familiar with the actual test. Because Ohio's state assessment is new to you, you may become scared. You may worry about the test, and this might interfere with your ability to show what you know.

This chapter offers tips you can use on Ohio's state assessment and many other tests. The ideas will build your test-taking confidence.

Worry Less About Tests

There are many things most of us would rather do than take a test. What would you rather do? Go to recess? See a movie? Eat a snack? Go swimming? Take a test? Most of us would not choose "take a test." This doesn't mean we're afraid of tests. It means we like to do things that are more fun!

Some students do not want to take tests for another reason. They are afraid of tests and are afraid of failing. Even though they are smart enough to do well, they are scared. All of us worry about a test at one time or another. So, if you worry about tests, you are not alone.

When people worry about tests or are scared of tests, they have what is called "test stress." You may have heard your parents say, "I'm feeling really stressed today." That means they have worried feelings. These feelings of stress can get in the way of doing your best. When you have test stress, it will be harder to show what you know. This chapter will help you get over your stress and worry less. You won't be scared. You will feel calm, happy, and proud.

If your mind is a mess

Because of terrible stress,

And you feel that you can't change at all.

Just pick up this book,

And take a look,

Our tips won't let you fall!

It's OK to Worry a Little Bit

Most people worry a little bit about something. Worrying isn't always a bad thing. A small amount of worrying is helpful. If you worry about crossing the street, you are more careful. When you worry about your schoolwork, you work hard to do it right. As you can see, a little worrying isn't bad. However, you have to make sure you don't let worrying get in the way of doing your best. Think about crossing the street. If you worry too much, you'll never go anywhere. You can see how worrying too much is not a good thing.

Third graders have a very special job. That job is taking Ohio's state assessment. The people who give the assessment want to know what you're learning in school. All children in Ohio are terrific and can learn to do their best on Ohio's state assessment without worrying too much or too little.

What Kind of Kid Are You?

Test stress and worrying too much or too little can get in your way. The good news is there are ways you can help yourself do better on tests. All you have to do is change the way you think about taking tests. You can do better, not just by learning more or studying more, but by changing the way you think about things.

Now you will read about some students who changed the way they think about tests. You may see that these students have some of the same feelings you have. You will learn how each of these kids faced a problem and ended up doing better on tests.

Stay-Away Stephanie

Stephanie thought that it was better to stay away from tests than to try at all. She was scared to face tests. She thought, "If I stay home sick, I won't have to take the test. I don't care if I get in trouble; I'm just not going to take the test." Stay-Away Stephanie felt less nervous when she ran away from tests, but she never learned to face her fear. Stephanie's teacher thought Stephanie didn't care about tests or school, but this wasn't true at all. Stay-Away Stephanie really worried about tests. She stayed away instead of trying to face each challenge.

One day, Stephanie's mom had an idea! "Stephanie, do you remember when you were afraid to ride your bike after I took the training wheels off?" her mom said. "You would hide whenever I wanted to take a bike ride. You said, 'I would rather walk than learn to ride a two-wheel bike.'" Stephanie knew that wasn't true. She wanted to learn to ride her bike, but she was scared. She stayed away from the challenge. When Stephanie faced her fear, step by step, she learned to ride her bike. "Stephanie," her mom said, "I think you stay away from tests because you're worried." Stephanie knew her mom was right. She had to face tests step by step.

Stephanie and her teacher came up with a plan. First, Stephanie's teacher gave her two test questions to do in school. For homework, Stephanie did two more questions. When Stephanie was scared, she talked with her mom or her teacher. She didn't stay away. Soon, Stephanie knew how to ask for help, and she took tests without being worried. Now, she has a new nickname: "Super-Successful Stephanie!"

If you are like Stay-Away Stephanie, talk with your teacher or someone who can help you. Together, you can learn to take tests one step at a time. You will be a successful student instead of a stay-away student.

Worried Wendy

Wendy always thought that the worst would happen. Her mind worried about everything. "What if I can't answer all the questions? What if I don't do well? My teacher won't like me. My dad will be upset. I will have to study a lot more." Wendy spent her time worrying. Instead, she should have learned to do well on tests.

Wendy was so worried her stomach hurt. Wendy's doctor knew she wasn't sick; she was worried. "Wendy," he said, "I have known you ever since you were born. You have always been curious. You wanted to know how everything worked and where everything was. But now your curious mind is playing tricks on you. You are so worried, you're making yourself sick."

Wendy's doctor put a clock on his desk. "Look at this clock. Is it a good clock or a bad clock?" Wendy had no answer. "Believe it or not, Wendy, we can trick our minds into thinking it is good or bad. I'm going to say bad things about this clock as fast as I can. First, it's not very big. Also, because the clock is small, I might not read the time on it correctly. Since the clock is so small, I might lose it forever." Wendy agreed it was a bad clock. "But wait," said her doctor. "I think the clock is a neat shape, and I like the colors. I like having it in my office; it tells time well. It didn't cost much, so if I lose it, it isn't a big deal." Wendy realized she could look at tests the way the doctor looked at the clock. You don't have to worry. You can see good things, not bad.

Critical Carlos

Carlos always put himself down. He thought he failed at everything he did. If he got a B+ on his homework, he would say, "I made so many mistakes, I didn't get an A." He never said good things like, "I worked hard. I'm proud of my B+." Carlos didn't do well on tests because he told himself, "I don't do well on anything, especially tests."

Last week, Carlos got a 95% on a test about lakes and rivers. Carlos stared at his paper. He was upset. "What is the matter, Carlos?" his teacher asked. "Is something wrong?" Carlos replied, "I'm stupid; I missed five points. I should have gotten a 100%."

"Carlos, nobody's perfect: not me, not you, not anybody. I think 95 out of 100 is super! It's not perfect, but it is very good. Celebrate, Carlos!" Carlos smiled; he knew his teacher was right. Now, Carlos knows he has to feel good about what he does. He isn't sad about his mistakes. He's cheerful, not critical.

Look at the chart below. Use this chart to find out all the good things about yourself. Some examples are given to get you started.

Good Things About Me
1. *I make my grandmother happy when I tell her a joke.*
2. *I taught my dog how to shake hands.*
3. *I can do two somersaults in a row.*
4.
5.
6.

Victim Vince

Vince couldn't take responsibility for himself. He said everything was someone else's fault. "Ohio's state assessment is too hard. I won't do well because they made the test too hard. And, last night, my little brother made so much noise I couldn't write my story. It's his fault I won't do well. I asked Mom to buy my favorite snack. I have to have it when I study. She forgot to pick it up at the store. I can't study without my snack. It's her fault." Vince complained and complained.

Vince's aunt told him he had to stop blaming everyone for his troubles. "You can make a difference, Vince," she said. "When is your next test?" Vince told her he had a spelling test on Friday. "You're going to be the boss of the test. First, let's pick a time to study. How is every day at 4:00 p.m.?" Vince agreed. "Now, how are you going to study?"

"I like to practice writing the words a couple of times," Vince said. "Then, I ask Mom or Dad to quiz me."

"Great idea. Every day at 4:00 p.m., you're going to write each word four times. Then, ask one of your parents to review your list. You're the boss of the spelling test, Vince, because you have a plan."

Vince's Study Plan

Time	Monday	Tuesday	Wednesday	Thursday	Friday
					Spelling Test
4:00	Write down spelling words. Then, ask Mom or Dad to help.	Write down spelling words. Then, ask Mom or Dad to help.	Write down spelling words. Then, ask Mom or Dad to help.	Write down spelling words. Then, ask Mom or Dad to help.	
4:30					
5:00					
5:30					
6:00					
7:00	Look at spelling words again.	Look at spelling words again.	Look at spelling words again.	Look at spelling words again.	
7:30					Get a movie for doing well!

When Friday came, Vince's whole world changed. Instead of being in a bad mood because of a poor grade, Vince felt powerful! He took his spelling test and scored an A-. Vince could not believe his eyes! His teacher was thrilled. Vince soon learned he could control his attitude. Vince is no longer a victim. Instead, he is "Victor Vince."

Perfect Pat

Pat spent all her time studying. She told herself, "I should study more. I should write this book report over. I should study every minute for Ohio's state assessment." Trying hard is fine, but Pat worked so much, she never felt she had done enough. Pat always thought she should be studying. Pat would play with her friends, but she never had a good time. In the middle of kickball or crafts, Pat thought, "I should be preparing for Ohio's state assessment. I should be writing my book report." When Pat took a test, she worried about each question. "I can't answer this one. I should have studied harder."

"Pat," her principal said, "you have to relax. You're not enjoying school." Pat replied, "I can't do that. There is so much more to learn." The principal gave Pat some tips on how to use her study time better.

- Do not study for long periods of time. Instead, try to work for about 10–20 minutes at a time, and then take a break. Everyone needs a break!

- Ask yourself questions as you go along. After you study a fact, test yourself to see if you remember it. As you read, ask yourself questions about what you are reading. Think about what you are studying!

- Find a special time to study. You may want to think of a good time to study with the help of your parents or your teacher. You could choose to study from 4:30 to 5:00 every day after school. After dinner, you could work from 7:30 to 8:00. After you finish studying, do not worry! You have done a lot for a third grader.

- Remember, you are a third-grade kid! School is very important, but playing, having fun, and being with your friends and family are also very important parts of growing up. Having fun does not mean you won't do well in school. It doesn't mean you will do poorly on Ohio's state assessment either. Having fun in your life makes you a happier person and helps you do better on tests.

Everyone Else Is Better Edward

Edward worried about everyone else. During holidays, Edward thought about the presents other people received. At his baseball game, he worried his teammates would score more runs. Edward always wanted to know how his friends did on tests. He spent so much time worrying about what other people were doing, he forgot to pay attention to his own studying and test taking.

"Edward, you're not going to succeed if you don't worry about yourself," his grandfather told him. "You need to start talking about what you can do. Instead of asking your friend how he did on a test, you say, 'I got an 85%. Next time, I want to get a 90%.' " When Edward practiced this, he worried less about tests and was a whole lot happier.

Shaky Sam

Sam was great at sports. He was friendly and funny, and he had many friends. However, Sam had one big problem. Every time he thought about taking a test, he would start shaking inside. His heart would start pounding like a drum. His stomach would get upset. Even the night before a test, he started shaking really hard.

Sam's older brother liked to sing. He told Sam he used to get nervous before he sang to a crowd of people. "Sam, you need to trick your body. Don't think about the test; think about something fun and happy."

Sam closed his eyes. He thought about making four shots in a row on the basketball court. He thought about his favorite dessert: vanilla ice cream. He thought about swimming in his neighbor's pool. When he opened his eyes, he wasn't shaking.

Practice thinking happy thoughts, and make believe you are far away from your troubles. Test stress will disappear.

Other Ways That Third Graders Have Stopped Worrying About Tests

Third graders are pretty smart kids. They have lots of good ideas for getting rid of test stress. Here are some ideas from other third graders.

- When I am scared or worried, I talk to my neighbor. She is 70 years old. She is the smartest person I know. We sit on her porch and eat cookies and talk. It makes me feel better to know she had some of the same problems when she was in third grade. She did well in school, and I know I can, too.

- Everything is harder in third grade, especially reading and math. I didn't want to go to school. I talked to my teacher, and he said we should have a talk every day before class. We talk about my homework, and he gives me tips. This really calms me down. When I am calm, I always do better.

- I used to worry that I wasn't doing well in school. I thought everyone else was smarter. My dad gave me a special folder. I keep all my tests in it. When I look at the tests, I see how much I have learned. I know I am doing a good job.

Ohio kids are smart kids! You, your teachers, and your family and friends can help you find other ways to beat test stress. You will be surprised how much you know and how well you will do on Ohio's state assessment.

Test-Taking Hints for Test Heroes

Introduction

Many third graders have not seen a test like Ohio's state assessment where they have to fill in answer bubbles or write answers on lines. Before you sit down to take a test, it is a good idea to review problem-solving and test-taking strategies. The words "test-taking strategies" may be difficult to understand, so this chapter is called Test-Taking Hints for Test Heroes.

This chapter offers many hints you can use when you take Ohio's state assessment and other tests. The ideas will build your confidence and improve your test-taking skills.

Do Your Best: Think Like a Genius!

Most third graders think the smartest kids do the best on tests. Smart kids may do well on tests, but all kids can do their best. By learning some helpful hints, most kids can do better than they ever thought they could on tests!

Learning to do well on tests will be helpful to you throughout your whole life, not just in third grade. Kids who are "test smart" feel very good about themselves. They have an "I can do it" feeling about themselves. This feeling helps them succeed in school, in sports, and in music. It even helps with making friends. Test-smart kids usually do well in their schoolwork, too. They believe they can do anything!

Become an Awesome Test Hero!

1. Fill In the Answer Bubble

You will use a pencil to take Ohio's state assessment. Think about tests you have taken. To answer questions, you may have written an answer, circled the correct answer, or solved a math problem. Ohio's state assessment is different. You will use your pencil to fill in answer bubbles. The test is mostly multiple choice, but there are a few short-answer and extended-response questions for which you will write your answer on lines.

For each multiple-choice question, you will have three choices to pick from. After you read the question and all the answer choices, think about which choice is correct. Next to each choice, you will see an answer bubble. The answer bubbles are not very big. They are smaller than the end of an eraser, smaller than a dime, and smaller than a jellybean. Even though the answer bubbles are small, they are very important! To answer each question, you must fill in the answer bubble next to the correct choice. Only fill in one answer bubble for each multiple-choice question. Fill in the bubble all the way, and do not color outside the bubble. Make sure you fill in the answer bubble neatly when you take Ohio's state assessment.

Look at the example below. You can see the correct way to fill in an answer bubble. Practice filling in the answer bubbles in this example.

There was a girl named Devine,
Who thought that a dot was a line!
She didn't fill in the bubble;
She was really in trouble!
When her answers are wrong she will whine!

Correct: ● Incorrect: ✓ ✗ ● ▰ ◐

Practice filling in the answer bubbles here: ○ ○ ○ ○ ○

Learning how to fill in answer bubbles takes practice, practice, and more practice! It may not be how you are used to marking the correct answer, but it is one way to give a right answer on Ohio's state assessment. Think about Kay!

A stubborn girl named Kay,
Liked to answer questions her own way.
So her marked answer bubbles,
Gave her all sorts of troubles.
Her test scores ruined her day!

You will also have to answer short-answer and extended-response questions. These are questions for which you have to fill in the answer. Some questions will only require one or two words or short phrases, but other questions may require a full sentence or two. Remember to write clearly and neatly so that people can read what you have written. Correct spelling and proper grammar will help make your response clear. However, if you misspell a word or forget to use a comma or period, it will not be counted against you. The most important thing to remember when you answer short-answer and extended-response questions is to completely answer the question as best you can.

2. Only Fill In the Answer Bubbles You Need To

It is not a good idea to touch the answer bubbles with your pencil until you are ready to fill in the right answer. If you put marks on more than one answer bubble, the computer that grades your test won't know which choice you think is right. Sometimes, kids get a little worried during the test. They might play with their pencils and tap their answer booklets. This is not a good idea. Look at all the answer choices. Only fill in one answer bubble for each multiple-choice question. This should be the answer bubble for the choice you think is right. Do not put marks in any other answer bubbles.

> There was a nice girl named Sue,
> Who thought she knew what to do.
> She marked all the spots.
> Her paper was covered with dots!
> And she didn't show all that she knew.

3. Think Good Thoughts

The better you feel about taking tests, the better you will do. Imagine you are a famous sports hero. You feel good about playing your favorite sport. You feel good about yourself. As a sports hero, you don't start a soccer game, football game, baseball game, tennis match, or swimming meet by saying, "This is going to be hard. I can't do it." Instead you say, "This may be a little hard, but I can do it. I am glad I have a chance to do this. I am going to do my best. I know I can." You may think Ohio's state assessment is a little hard, but you can do it. When you start Ohio's state assessment, remember to think good thoughts. This will help you to be the best test hero you can be.

> There was a girl named Gail,
> Who thought she always would fail.
> She said, "Tests are tough,
> I'm not smart enough."
> She had a sad end to her tale.

4. What Happens if I Don't Do Well on the Test?

Ohio's state assessment is one way to find out how much you have learned by the third grade. It is important to try your best on Ohio's state assessment, but remember, your friends, parents, and teachers will like you no matter how you do on this test.

> There was a nice boy named Chad,
> Who thought if he failed he was bad.
> His teacher said, "That's not true.
> I like you no matter how you do."
> Now Chad is glad and not sad.

5. Don't Be Too Scared or Too Calm

Being too scared about tests will get in the way of doing your best. If you are scared, you won't be able to think clearly. If you are scared, your mind can't focus on the test. You think about other things. Your body might start to feel nervous. There is a chapter in this book called Worry Less About Tests. It will help you feel calmer about tests. Read that chapter so you can feel calmer about Ohio's state assessment and other tests.

If you are too calm before taking a test, you might not do well. Sometimes, kids say, "I don't care about this!" They might not have pride in their schoolwork. They may be nervous. They may think Ohio's state assessment is "no big deal" and may try to forget about it. If you do not think a test is important and you try to forget about it, you are not thinking good thoughts. Don't be scared of the test, but don't forget about it. You can become a test hero and do your best if you take pride in your work.

There was a student named Claire
Who usually said, "I don't care."
Her sister named Bess,
Always felt total stress.
They weren't a successful pair!

6. Don't Rush; Speeding Through the Test Doesn't Help

The last time you took a test, did you look around the room to see who finished first? If someone handed his or her paper in before you, did you feel like you needed to hurry up? Kids feel that way sometimes, but rushing through questions will not help you on Ohio's state assessment. Finishing the assessment first, or second, or even third is not important. This may be a surprise to learn. Usually, we think speed is good. We hear about the fastest computer, the fastest runner, and the fastest car. Speed is exciting to think about, but working fast on the assessment will not make your test score better. Take your time, and you will be able to show what you know!

There was a third grader named Liz,
Who sped through her test like a whiz.
She thought she should race
At a very fast pace,
But it caused her to mess up her quiz.

7. Read Directions Carefully!

One of the best ways to become a test hero is to read directions. Directions help you understand what you're supposed to do. On Ohio's state assessment, it is really important to take your time and to read directions. You may say, "Why should I read directions? I know what to do." Here's a story that may change your mind.

Imagine you are a famous baker. Everyone thinks you make the best cakes in Ohio! One day, a group of kings and queens comes to Ohio for an important visit. They ask you to bake a special cake for them. You have never baked this type of cake before. The kings and queens give you directions, but you don't read them. You think to yourself, "Who has time? I don't need directions. I know how to bake cakes." You don't read the directions but put them in a drawer. This is not a good idea. The directions tell you to bake the special cake at 250 degrees, but you bake the cake at 350 degrees! What do you get? A very crispy cake and very angry kings and queens. You should have read the directions!

Make sure you read directions slowly and repeat them to yourself. You should understand the directions before you begin the test.

There was a nice boy named Fred,
Who ignored almost all that he read.
The directions were easy,
But he said, "I don't need these!"
He should have read them instead.

8. Don't Get Stuck on One Question

Some of the questions on Ohio's state assessment will be easy. Other questions might be a little harder. Don't let that worry you! If there is a question you're not sure how to answer, use your pencil to put a mark by the question. Remember, mark the question, not the answer choice bubbles. Once you have marked the hard question, move on to the next question. When you get to the end of the test, go back and try to answer the hard question. Once you have answered many easy questions, you might be able to answer the hard question with no problem.

If you mark a question and move on, you won't "get stuck." This is a good hint. Ohio's state assessment has lots of questions, so you will be able to show what you know. If there is a question that puzzles your mind, just go back to it later.

There was a sweet girl named Von,
Who got stuck and just couldn't go on.
She'd sit there and stare,
But the answer wasn't there.
Before she knew it, all the time was gone.

9. Use What You Know!

By the time you take Ohio's state assessment, you will have been in school for four years. You went to kindergarten, first grade, and second grade, and now you are in the third grade. You were taught lots of things in school, but you learned many things in other places, too. You may have gathered information at the library, in a magazine, from TV, from your parents, and from lots of other places. Third graders have a lot of information in their brains!

Sometimes, third graders forget how much they know. You may see a question that your teacher has not talked about. This is OK. You may have heard about it somewhere else. Take a minute to think about all you know.

Let's say you were asked the following question.

Melissa and her family go to Florida for a vacation. Melissa is excited about going to the beach and to an amusement park. She also really enjoys fresh orange juice. Melissa wants to walk to a store to buy an orange juice treat. The sign says the store is 200 yards away. If Melissa walks to the store, about how long will it take her?

○ A. about 5 minutes
○ B. about 30 minutes
○ C. about 1 hour

This seems like a hard question. You don't know how far 200 yards is. Stop and think for minute! You have heard the word "yard" before, but where? You may have heard it used in a football game; a football field is 100 yards. So 200 yards is about the length of two football fields. You know it will not take long to walk that far. Now you know the right answer; it will probably only take about 5 minutes. Even though you thought you didn't know the answer, you used the information you remembered from other places. You're on your way to becoming a test hero!

There was a boy named Drew,
Who forgot to use what he knew.
He had lots of knowledge.
He could have been in college,
But his correct answers were very few.

10. Luck Isn't Enough!

Have you ever had a lucky number, a lucky color, or even a lucky hat? Everyone believes in luck. A famous football player always wears the same shoes game after game because he thinks they give him good luck. This doesn't make any sense. Wearing old, smelly shoes doesn't help him play well. But he believes in luck anyway. Believing in luck can be fun, but it is not going to help you do well on Ohio's state assessment. The best way to do well is to PRACTICE! Listening to your teacher, practicing the hints you have learned in this book, and learning every day in the third grade will help you do your best.

> There was a cool boy named Chuck,
> Who thought taking tests was just luck.
> He never prepared.
> He said, "I'm not scared."
> When his test scores appear, he should duck!

11. Recheck Your Answers

Everyone makes mistakes. Checking your work is very important. There once was a famous magician. He was very good at what he did, but he never checked his work. One night, he was getting ready for a big magic show. There were hundreds of people watching the show. The magician's wife said, "Check your pockets for everything you need." The magician didn't listen. "I've done this a million times," he said to himself. "I don't need to check my pockets." What a bad idea! When he got on stage, he reached his hand into an empty pocket—no magic tricks! Next time, he will recheck his pockets to do the best job possible!

Going back and checking your work is very important. You can read a paragraph over again if there is something that you do not understand or something you forget. You will not be wasting time if you recheck your work. It is important to show what you know, not to show how fast you can go. Making sure you have put down the right answer is a good idea.

> There was a quick girl named Jen,
> Who read stuff once and never again.
> It would have been nice
> If she'd reread it twice.
> Her scores would have been better then!

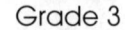

Helpful Hints from Other Third-Grade Test Heroes!

Third graders all over Ohio have good ideas about tests. Here are some of them!

- Ask yourself, "Did I answer the question that was asked?" Carefully read the question so you can give the right answer.

- Read each answer choice before filling in an answer bubble. Sometimes, you read the first choice, and it seems right. But, when you get to the third choice, you realize that's the correct answer. If you had stopped with the first choice, you would have answered the question incorrectly. It is important to read all three choices before answering the question.

- Remember, Ohio's state assessment is not trying to trick you! Do not look for trick answers. There will always be a right answer. If the answer choices do not look right, mark the question and go back to it later.

- Don't look around the room! Don't worry about how fast your friends are working, and don't worry about how well they are doing. Only worry about yourself. If you do that, you will do better on the test.

Reading

Introduction

In the Reading section of Ohio's state assessment, you will be asked questions to test what you have learned so far in school. These questions are based on the reading skills you have been taught in school through third grade. The questions you will answer are not meant to confuse or trick you, but are written so you have the best chance to show what you know.

Questions I Will Answer on Ohio's State Assessment

You will answer multiple-choice, short-answer, and extended-response questions on the Reading assessment. Multiple-choice items have three answer choices, and only one is correct. Short-answer items will require you to write a word, a phrase, or a sentence. Extended-response items will require you to write a few phrases, or a complete sentence or two.

The questions are based on reading selections. The selections may be literary or expository. Literary selections are fiction. Expository selections are informative.

Examples of an expository selection, a multiple-choice item, a short-answer item, and an extended-response item are shown below and on the following page.

A Sign of Pride

An important sign of the United States is our flag. Our flag stands for the land. It stands for the people. It stands for the government.

On June 14, 1777, the Continental Congress decided on one flag for the United States that would have 13 stripes. The stripes would be red and white. The first stripe would be red. The next stripe would be white. The stripe after that would be red, and so on. The Continental Congress also said the flag would have a group of 13 white stars on a blue background. The 13 stripes stood for the first 13 colonies. These 13 colonies were the first states in the United States. The 13 stars stood for the number of states in the United States at that time.

1. What colors were the stripes on the 1777 flag?

    ○ A. red and blue

    ● B. red and white

    ○ C. white and blue

2. In 1777, the Continental Congress decided the United States flag would have specific numbers of stars and stripes. List the correct number for each item listed below.

Stars and Stripes in 1777	How Many
Red Stripes in 1777	7
White Stripes in 1777	6
White Stars in 1777	13

3. Using information from the reading selection, list four reasons why the flag is an important sign of the United States?

A. The flag is a sign of pride.

B. The flag stands for the land.

C. The flag stands for the people.

D. The flag stands for the government.

Item Distribution on Ohio's State Assessment for Grade 3 Reading

Number of Items	36 or 37
Number of Multiple-Choice Questions	29
Number of Short-Answer Questions	4 or 6
Number of Extended-Response Questions	2 or 3
Types of Passages	2 Informational Texts 2 Literary Texts
Length of Passages	2 short (up to 350 words) 2 medium (351–500 words)

Note: This is the Item Distribution that will be used on the actual assessment for Grade 3 Reading. Each practice test in this book contains 40 questions.

Scoring

The Reading questions are based on four reading selections. The selections may be literary or expository. Literary selections are fictional. Expository selections are informative.

You will answer multiple-choice, short-answer, and extended-response questions in the Reading assessment. Multiple-choice items have three answer choices, and only one is correct. Short-answer items will require you to write a word, a phrase, or a sentence. Extended-response items will require you to write a few phrases, or a complete sentence or two.

Multiple-Choice Items

Multiple-choice items are used whenever a single, concise answer to the item is possible. The multiple-choice questions on Ohio's state assessment for Grade 3 Reading emphasize critical thinking over factual recollection. The multiple-choice items are worth one point each. There is no penalty for guessing; an item with no response will be automatically counted as incorrect.

Short-Answer and Extended-Response Items

On the Reading assessment, item-specific rubrics are used for each constructed-response question (short answer or extended response). Conventions of writing (sentence structure, word choice, usage, grammar, spelling, and mechanics) will not affect the scoring of short-answer and extended-response items unless there is interference with the clear communication of ideas.

Short-Answer Scoring

Short-answer items require a brief written response. Student responses receive a score of 0, 1 or 2 points. Each short answer item has an item-specific scoring guideline. These written responses may require supporting work or explanations. The following general two-point scoring guideline for short answer items is used as a template to develop item-specific scoring guidelines for each individual short answer item.

A **2-point response** provides a complete interpretation and/or correct solution. It demonstrates a thorough understanding of the concept or task. It indicates logical reasoning and conclusions. It is accurate, relevant, and complete.

A **1-point response** provides evidence of a partial interpretation and/or solution process. It demonstrates an incomplete understanding of the concept or task. It contains minor flaws in reasoning. It neglects to address some aspect of the task.

A **Zero-point response** does not meet the criteria required to earn one point. The response indicates inadequate understanding of the task and/or the idea or concept needed to answer the item. It may only repeat information given in the test item. The response may provide an incorrect solution/response and the provided supportive information may be totally irrelevant to the item, or possibly, no other information is shown. The student may have written on a different topic or written "I don't know."

Extended-Response Scoring

Extended-response items require students to demonstrate understanding in depth. Student responses receive a score of 0, 1, 2, 3 or 4 points. Each extended-response item has an item-specific scoring guideline. These written responses may include explanations, appropriate charts, tables, graphs, or other graphic organizers. The following general four-point rubric for extended response items is used as a template to develop item-specific scoring guidelines for each individual extended-response item.

A **4-point response** provides essential aspects of a complete interpretation and/or a correct solution. The response thoroughly addresses the points relevant to the concept or task. It provides strong evidence that information reasoning, and conclusions have a definite logical relationship. It is clearly focused and organized, showing relevance to the concept, task and/or solution process.

A **3-point response** provides essential elements of an interpretation and/or a solution. It addresses the points relevant to the concept or task. It provides ample evidence that information, reasoning, and conclusions have a logical relationship. It is focused and organized, showing relevance to the concept, task, or solution process.

A **2-point response** provides a partial interpretation and/or solution. It somewhat addresses the points relevant to the concept or task. It provides some evidence that information, reasoning, and conclusions have a relationship. It is relevant to the concept and/or task, but there are gaps in focus and organization.

A **1-point response** provides an unclear, inaccurate interpretation and/or solution. It fails to address or omits significant aspects of the concept or task. It provides unrelated or unclear evidence that information, reasoning, and conclusions have a relationship. There is little evidence of focus or organization relevant to the concept, task and/or solution process.

Scoring

A **Zero-point response** does not meet the criteria required to earn one point. The response indicates inadequate understanding of the task and/or the idea or concept needed to answer the item. It may only repeat information given in the test item. The response may provide an incorrect solution/response and the provided supportive information may be totally irrelevant to the item, or possibly, no other information is shown. The student may have written on a different topic or written "I don't know."

Glossary

alliteration: Repeating the same sound at the beginning of several words in a phrase or sentence. For example, "The bees buzzed in the back of the blue barn."

adjectives: Words that describe nouns.

adverbs: Words that describe verbs.

antonyms: Words that mean the opposite (e.g., *light* is an antonym of *dark*).

audience: The people who read a written piece or hear the piece being read.

author's purpose: The reason an author writes, such as to entertain, to inform, or to persuade.

author's tone: The attitude the writer takes toward an audience, a subject, or a character. Tone is conveyed through the writer's choice of words and details. Examples of tone are happy, sad, angry, gentle, etc.

base word (also called root word): The central part of a word that other word parts may be attached to.

biography: A true story about a person's life.

cause: The reason for an action, feeling, or response.

character: A person or an animal in a story, play, or other literary work.

compare: To use examples to show how things are alike.

contrast: To use examples to show how things are different.

details: Many small parts which help to tell a story.

descriptive text: To create a clear picture of a person, place, thing, or idea by using vivid words.

directions: An order or instructions on how to do something or how to act.

draw conclusion: To make a decision or form an opinion after considering the facts from the text.

effect: A result of a cause.

events: Things that happen.

fact: An actual happening or truth.

Glossary

fiction: A passage that is made up rather than factually true. Examples of fiction are novels and short stories.

format: The way a published piece of writing looks, including the font, legibility, spacing, margins, and white space.

generalize: To come to a broad idea or rule about something after considering particular facts.

genres: Categories of literary and informational works (e.g., biography, mystery, historical fiction, poem).

graphic organizer: Any illustration, chart, table, diagram, map, etc., used to help interpret information about the text.

heading: A word or group of words at the top or front of a piece of writing.

infer: To make a guess based on facts and observations.

inference: An important idea or conclusion drawn from reasoning rather than directly stated in the text.

inform: To give knowledge; to tell.

informational text (also called expository text): Text with the purpose of telling about details, facts, and information that is true (nonfiction). Informational text is found in textbooks, encyclopedias, biographies, and newspaper articles.

literary devices: Techniques used to convey an author's message or voice (e.g., figurative language, similes, metaphors, etc.).

literary text (also called narrative text): Text that describes actions or events, usually written as fiction. Examples are novels and short stories.

main idea: The main reason the passage was written; every passage has a main idea. Usually you can find the main idea in the topic sentence of the paragraph.

metaphor: A comparison between two unlike things without using the words "like" or "as." An example of a metaphor is, "My bedroom is a junkyard!"

Glossary

mood: The feeling or emotion the reader gets from a piece of writing.

nonfiction: A passage of writing that tells about real people, events, and places without changing any facts. Examples of nonfiction are an autobiography, a biography, an essay, a newspaper article, a magazine article, a personal diary, and a letter.

onomatopoeia: The use of words in which the sounds of the word suggest the sound associated with it. For example, buzz, hiss, splat.

opinion: What one thinks about something or somebody; an opinion is not necessarily based on facts. Feelings and experiences usually help a person form an opinion.

passage: A passage or writing that may be fiction (literary/narrative) or nonfiction (informational/expository).

persuade: To cause to do something by using reason or argument; to cause to believe something.

plan: A method of doing something that has been thought out ahead of time.

plot: A series of events that make up a story. Plot tells "what happens" in a story, novel, or narrative poem.

plot sequence: The order of events in a story.

poetry: A type of writing that uses images and patterns to express feelings.

point of view: The way a story is told; it could be in first person, omniscient, or in third person.

predict: The ability of the reader to know or expect that something is going to happen in a text before it does.

prefix: A group of letters added to the beginning of a word. For example, untie, rebuild, preteen.

preposition: A word that links another word or group of words to other parts of the sentence. Examples are *in, on, of, at, by, between, outside,* etc.

prewriting: The thinking and planning the writer does before writing the actual draft.

Glossary

problem: An issue or question in a text that needs to be answered.

prompt: A writing task. In the OAT, students will be instructed to write to a specific topic, audience, purpose, and form (i.e., a letter, a paragraph, a story).

proofreading: Editing a written work.

published work: The final writing draft shared with the audience.

reliable: Sources used for writing that are trustworthy.

resource: A source of help or support.

revise: To rework your writing to improve it.

rhyme: When words have the same last sound. For example, hat/cat, most/toast, ball/call.

root word (also called base word): The central part of a word that other word parts may be attached to.

schema: The accumulated knowledge that a person can draw from life experiences to help understand concepts, roles, emotions, and events.

selected response: In the OAT, multiple-choice questions with three possible answer choices. The student will choose one correct answer from the three answer choices.

sentence: A group of words that express a complete thought. It has a subject and a verb.

sequential order: The arrangement or ordering of information, content, or ideas (e.g., a story told in chronological order describes what happened first, then second, then third, etc.).

setting: The time and place of a story or play. The setting helps to create the mood in a story, such as inside a spooky house or inside a shopping mall during the holidays.

simile: A comparison between two unlike things, using the words "like" or "as." "Her eyes are as big as saucers" is an example of a simile.

solution: An answer to a problem.

Glossary

stanzas: Lines of poetry grouped together.

story: An account of something that happened.

story elements: The important parts of the story, including characters, setting, plot, problem, and solution.

style: A way of writing that is individual to the writer, such as the writer's choice of words, phrases, and images.

suffix: A group of letters added to the end of a word. For example, teach<u>er</u>, color<u>ful</u>, sugar<u>less</u>, etc.

summary: To retell what happens in a story in a short way by telling the main ideas, not details.

supporting details: Statements that often follow the main idea. Supporting details give you more information about the main idea.

symbolism: Something that represents something else. For example, a dove is a symbol for peace.

synonyms: Words with the same, or almost the same, meaning.

theme: The major idea or topic that the author reveals in a literary work. A theme is usually not stated directly in the work. Instead, the reader has to think about all the details of the work and then make an inference (an educated guess) about what they all mean.

title: A name of a book, film, play, piece of music, or other work of art.

tone: A way of writing that conveys a feeling.

topic sentence: A sentence that states the main idea of the paragraph.

transition: Words that link ideas together.

valid: Correct, acceptable.

verb: A word that shows action or being.

voice: To express a choice or opinion.

word web: A graphic organizer created by the writer during prewriting. A web is used to gather and connect facts, ideas, concepts, and words.

Reading Practice Test 1

Reading R

Directions:

Today you will be taking a practice Reading assessment. This is a test of how well you understand what you read. The test consists of vocabulary questions and reading selections followed by questions about each reading selection. Three different types of questions appear on this test: multiple choice, short answer and extended response.

There are several important things to remember:

1. Read each reading selection carefully. You may look back at the reading selection as often as necessary. You may underline or mark parts of any selection.

2. Read each question carefully. Think about what is being asked. If a graph or other diagram goes with the question, look at it carefully to help you answer the question. Then choose or write the answer that you think is best.

3. When you write your answers, write them neatly and clearly in the space provided using a pencil.

4. When you answer a multiple choice question, make sure you fill in the circle next to the answer. Mark only one answer. If you do not know the answer to a question, skip it and go on. If you have time, go back to the questions you skipped and answer them before you hand in your Student Workbook.

6. If you finish the test early, you may check over your work. When you are finished and your Student Workbook has been collected, you may take out your silent work.

7. When you finish the test, you may not go on to, or look at the mathematics section of the Student Workbook.

Go to next page

Reading

Directions: Carefully read each question. Fill in the circle next to the correct answer.

1. Which word is an antonym for **damp**?

   ○ A. hot
   ○ B. dark
   ○ C. dry

2. Which word is a homonym for **right**?

   ○ A. sight
   ○ B. write
   ○ C. left

Directions: Read the selection.

A Sign of Pride

An important sign of the United States is our flag. Our flag stands for the land. It stands for the people. It stands for the government.

On June 14, 1777, the Continental Congress decided on one flag for the United States that would have 13 stripes. The stripes would be red and white. The first stripe would be red. The next stripe would be white. The stripe after that would be red, and so on. The Continental Congress also said the flag would have a group of 13 white stars on a blue background. The 13 stripes stood for the first 13 colonies. These 13 colonies were the first states in the United States. The 13 stars stood for the number of states in the United States at that time.

The Continental Congress did not say how the stars should be arranged. On some flags, 12 stars were placed in a circle with one star in the middle. On others, the 13 stars were placed in a circle.

As new states became part of the United States, more stars and stripes were added to the flag. People soon thought the flag had too many stripes. The Flag Act of 1818 stated that the American flag would only have 13 stripes, one stripe for each of the first 13 colonies. The Flag Act also said the American flag should have one white star for each state in the United States. In 1846, the flag had 28 stars. By 1861, the number of stars was 34. In 1898, the flag had 45 stars. The last change to the flag was in 1960. A star was added for the state of Hawaii. The flag with 50 stars is the one we use today.

The American flag has had several nicknames. Our country's earliest flag was known as the Continental flag, or the Congress colors. Today, it is called the Stars and Stripes. It is also called Old Glory or the Red, White, and Blue. No matter what name is used, the flag we see flying today is an important sign of pride for our country.

Directions: Use the selection to answer questions 3–11.

3. This sentence is from the selection.

   "The Flag Act of 1818 **stated** that the American flag would only have 13 stripes, one for each of the first 13 colonies."

   What does the word **stated** mean?

   ○ A. changed
   ○ B. said
   ○ C. showed

4. This sentence is from the selection.

   "The American flag has had several nicknames."

   What is a good guess of how many nicknames the flag has had?

   ○ A. one
   ○ B. six
   ○ C. a thousand

Reading

5. This sentence is from the selection.

   "Our country's **earliest** flag was known as the Continental flag, or the Congress colors."

   Which word is a synonym for **earliest**?

   ○ A. first
   ○ B. last
   ○ C. newest

6. Why does the American flag have 50 stars on it?

   _____

   _____

   How was it decided that the flag would have 50 stars?

   _____

   _____

7. Which of the following is not a nickname for the American flag?

   ○ A. Old Glory

   ○ B. Continental Congress

   ○ C. Stars and Stripes

8. What kind of selection is "A Sign of Pride"?

   ○ A. poem

   ○ B. folk tale

   ○ C. nonfiction

9. List two things that describe what the American flag looks like.

   a. _____

   _____

   b. _____

   _____

Go to next page

Reading

10. What do the 13 stripes on the flag stand for?

    ○ A. 13 original colonies

    ○ B. 13 states in the United States

    ○ C. 13 nicknames

11. Number the events in the order that they happened.

    ___ The American flag had 45 stars.

    ___ The American flag had 13 stars.

    ___ The American flag had 50 stars.

The Harrison Elementary Press
A Newspaper Written By Kids, For Kids

March Issue   Science Section, Page 1

FROGS AND TOADS
By Federico Garcia

It's important to look to see if the animal you are about to kiss is a frog or a toad. You may never find a handsome prince if you kiss the wrong amphibian. Can you tell the difference between a frog and a toad?

It is easy to confuse frogs and toads just by looking at them. They are both amphibians. This means they can live both in water and on land. They both are coldblooded. This means their body temperatures are the same as the air temperatures around them. They have to look for cool, shady places to rest if they become too hot. Frogs and toads look for warm, sunny places if they are too cold. Both animals are vertebrates. This means they have spines. Their body shape is almost the same. Their eyes stick out from their faces, so they can see in most directions without turning their heads.

Frogs and toads use their long, sticky tongues to catch insects to eat. Both frogs and toads swallow their food whole.

How are frogs and toads different? Frogs are better swimmers and jumpers because they have long back legs. A toad's back legs are shorter. Frogs are more likely to be found near water. Toads often live in drier places. Most frogs have four webbed feet. Toads do not have webs on their back feet. The skin of a frog is smooth and damp. Toads have drier skin that is covered with bumps called glands. Frogs have teeth in their upper jaws and no teeth in their lower jaws. Toads have no teeth at all.

As you can see, frogs and toads are not the same type of amphibian. Of course, a frog turning into a handsome prince only happens in fairy tales. Who would want to kiss a frog or a toad anyway?

Go to next page

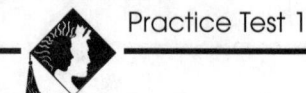

Reading

Directions: Use the selection to answer questions 12–20.

12. What is the title of this article?

    ○ A. Frogs and Toads
    ○ B. Science Section
    ○ C. The Harrison Elementary Press

13. Why did the author write this article?

    ○ A. to tell students that toads are better than frogs
    ○ B. to tell a story about a frog turning into a prince
    ○ C. to explain how frogs and toads are alike and different

14. Which sentence from the article helps you know this selection is nonfiction?

    ○ A. "It's important to look to see if the animal you are about to kiss is a frog or a toad."
    ○ B. "Both animals are vertebrates."
    ○ C. "You may never find a handsome prince if you kiss the wrong amphibian."

Go to next page

15. A third-grade class decides to make an informational chart about frogs using the information from this article. Which item would probably not be found on the class' chart?

   A. ○ Frogs are good swimmers.
   B. ○ Frogs have smooth, damp skin.
   C. ○ Frogs can turn into princes.

16. List four examples of how frogs and toads are alike. Use information from the reading selection in your answer.

   a. _____

   b. _____

   c. _____

   d. _____

Reading

17. What is the suffix of **jumpers**?

    ○ A. -ers

    ○ B. jump-

    ○ C. jumpers

18. How do frogs and toads catch insects to eat?

    ○ A. turn their heads

    ○ B. use their long, sticky tongues

    ○ C. use their teeth

19. List two ways toads are different from frogs. Use information from the reading selection in your answer.

a. _____

_____

b. _____

_____

20. In fairy tales, what happens if you kiss a frog?

○ A. It turns into a toad.

○ B. It turns into a tree.

○ C. It turns into a handsome prince.

Tony's Skunk

Tony had never been so scared. The light of his flashlight was shining on a small animal. The bright eyes of a skunk stared at him. "You're smaller than my puppy," he whispered. He knew the animal wouldn't attack him. Yet he was afraid to move. "What am I going to do?" he thought. Tony knew if he did the wrong thing, he would be very sorry.

Tony had played in the woods near his house many times, but this was the first time he had seen a skunk. Tony didn't know much about the black and white animal. He did know that he must be careful. When skunks are scared, they spray something that smells bad. It is for protection. This smell keeps away other animals that might want to eat the skunk. Tony knew the skunk would make a noise and pound its feet if it was very scared. So he carefully watched the little animal.

The skunk seemed surprised. "He's as scared as I am," Tony thought. Tony's eyes were locked on the skunk. The skunk's eyes stared at Tony. A few more minutes passed. Tony was ready to do something. "I hope I'm doing the right thing."

Tony began to move away slowly. He never let his eyes leave the skunk. He picked up his right foot, then his left. He softly whispered to the skunk, "I don't want to hurt you. Just let me get away from you."

The skunk was still. Tony moved away from him. Inch by inch, Tony backed away through the woods. He didn't want to move his flashlight off the skunk. He couldn't see where he was walking. He hoped he didn't trip and fall. The leaves softly crunched under his feet. The skunk remained still.

He started to feel better. Tony was about 12 feet from the little animal. He kept walking gently. Then, suddenly, his foot came down and "CRACK!" The sound was very loud. It was only a dry stick, but it made Tony jump. The flashlight hit the ground. Light bounced around the woods. Tony's heart was beating fast. He couldn't see the skunk. The light no longer hit the skunk's eyes. Tony heard the skunk make a noise. "Oh no! I'm going to get it!" But Tony was lucky. The skunk had different plans. Tony heard four small footsteps in the leaves. "That was a close one," Tony thought. He picked up his flashlight and quickly headed in the other direction.

Reading

Directions: Use the selection to answer questions 21–30.

21. What happens after Tony steps on the dry stick?

    ○ A. Tony sees the skunk.

    ○ B. Tony drops his flashlight.

    ○ C. Tony's foot hurts.

22. Why is Tony scared?

    ○ A. He thinks the skunk might bite him.

    ○ B. He thinks the skunk might spray him.

    ○ C. He is lost in the woods.

23. How does Tony try to solve his problem with the skunk?

    ○ A. He throws his flashlight at the skunk.

    ○ B. He slowly steps away from the skunk.

    ○ C. He cracks a stick to scare the skunk.

24. This sentence is from the selection.

    "He kept walking **gently**."

    What does the word **gently** mean?

    ○ A. not gentle

    ○ B. less gentle

    ○ C. in a gentle way

25. What is the most likely reason Tony is carrying a flashlight?

    ○ A. It is dark outside.

    ○ B. It is sunny outside.

    ○ C. It is windy outside.

Reading

26. What will Tony probably tell his friends about playing in the woods near his house?

   ○ A. He will tell them to play there only at night.

   ○ B. He will tell them to be careful because they might run into a skunk.

   ○ C. He will tell them that the skunks in the woods are not dangerous.

27. Why does Tony move away from the skunk so slowly?

   ○ A. He doesn't want the skunk to see him.

   ○ B. He doesn't want the skunk to run away.

   ○ C. He doesn't want to scare the skunk.

28. Fill in the web with ideas from the selection about what skunks do when they are scared.

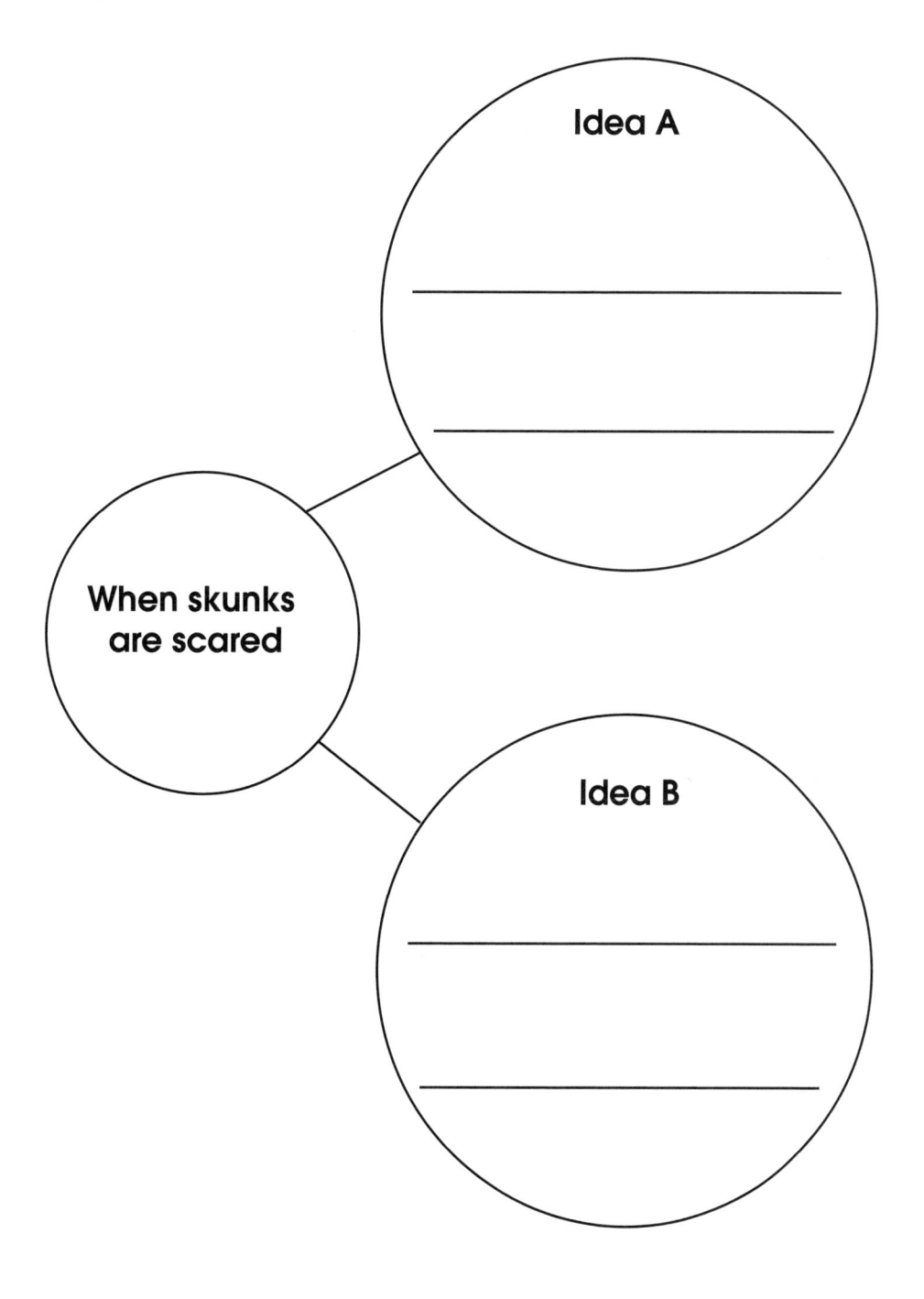

Idea A
_____
_____

When skunks are scared

Idea B
_____
_____

Reading

29. These sentences are from the selection.

    "Then, suddenly, his foot came down and "CRACK!" The sound was very loud. It was only a dry stick, but it made Tony jump. The flashlight hit the ground. Light bounced around the woods. Tony's heart was beating fast. He couldn't see the skunk. The light no longer hit the skunk's eyes. Tony heard the skunk make a noise."

    How does the author want you to feel as you read these sentences?

    ○ A. excited and a little scared

    ○ B. sad and angry

    ○ C. tired and hungry

30. This sentence is from the selection.

    "The skunk was **still**."

    Which word or words are a synonym for **still**?

    ○ A. moving fast

    ○ B. not moving

    ○ C. skipping

Birds of a Feather

It was a quiet Monday morning on Feathertree Lane. Spring had arrived. The race was on. Who would have the best nests this year? It was the only thing the birds of the neighborhood could think about. Mrs. Sparrow flew down the street. She watched the other birds from the neighborhood gathering sticks and grass for their nests.

Mrs. Sparrow landed at a bird feeder to have a snack. She picked up a bite of her favorite birdseed. Then, one of her neighbors, Mrs. Jay, landed next to her. "Have you talked to the new neighbors yet?" Mrs. Sparrow asked.

"No, I haven't, but I can see they've been busy. Have you seen the nest they're building? It's beautiful," Mrs. Jay replied.

"Yes, it seems to be quite a nest. I wonder where they got the idea. I've never seen a bird who could weave grasses together in the way that they have."

Mrs. Jay wiped some birdseed from her beak before she answered. "They do seem to be good at building nests. I've been watching. They are so close to my nest. Their nest might be the biggest one in our neighborhood. But I'm quite happy in our nest. My husband, Blue, did a wonderful job finding the right grasses, sticks, bark, and feathers for our nest this year. It may not be the largest, but it is just right for our family. I'm very proud of our home."

"As you should be," said Mrs. Sparrow. "It does look quite cozy. Do you remember two years ago when the Hummingbird family made their nest here? It was so tiny. It was even smaller than my home."

"That's true," Mrs. Jay chirped. "They were always humming while they worked. I wondered if they had forgotten the words to their songs."

Mrs. Sparrow laughed. "No, no, no. The humming came from their wings moving so fast. But I never thought they were very friendly. And the Robins! They're not so nice! Just because they have those beautiful red feathers doesn't mean they should be mean. Look at the Cardinals. They have beautiful red feathers, too. They don't fly away when another bird comes by the feeder. They'll talk to any bird in the neighborhood. Besides, I think we're all beautiful in our own ways. Don't you?"

"Yes, I do agree with you. Oh, no! The people in the yellow house let their dog out. When he sees us, we won't be able to hear ourselves chirp. I think I'll head back to my nest rather than listen to him. I'll see you later, Mrs. Sparrow." Mrs. Jay chirped her goodbye and flew away.

Mrs. Sparrow ate another seed before she heard the barking begin. "There goes the neighborhood," she thought to herself as she flew home.

Directions: Use the selection to answer questions 31–40.

31. Look at the diagram about the Robins and the Cardinals.

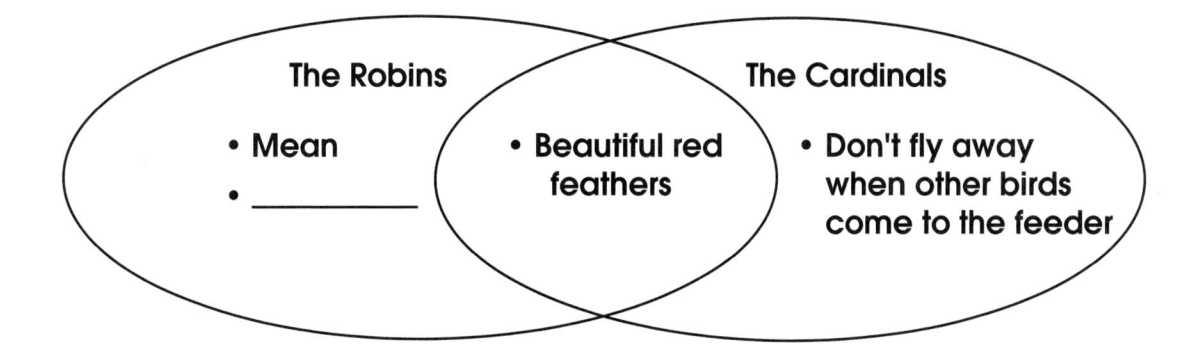

```
   The Robins              The Cardinals
   • Mean      • Beautiful red    • Don't fly away
   • _____      feathers           when other birds
                                    come to the feeder
```

Which of the following goes in the blank?

○ A. Fly away every time another bird comes by the feeder

○ B. Hum while they work

○ C. Will talk to any bird in the neighborhood

Reading

32. What happens before Mrs. Jay lands at the bird feeder?

   ○ A. The people in the yellow house let their dog outside.

   ○ B. Mrs. Sparrow watches her neighbors gather sticks and grass.

   ○ C. Mrs. Sparrow asks about the new neighbors.

33. Which event happens last?

   ○ A. The dog from the yellow house starts barking.

   ○ B. Mrs. Sparrow eats another seed.

   ○ C. Mrs. Sparrow says the Cardinals have beautiful red feathers.

34. Read the chart below. It shows the order in which some events happened in the story.

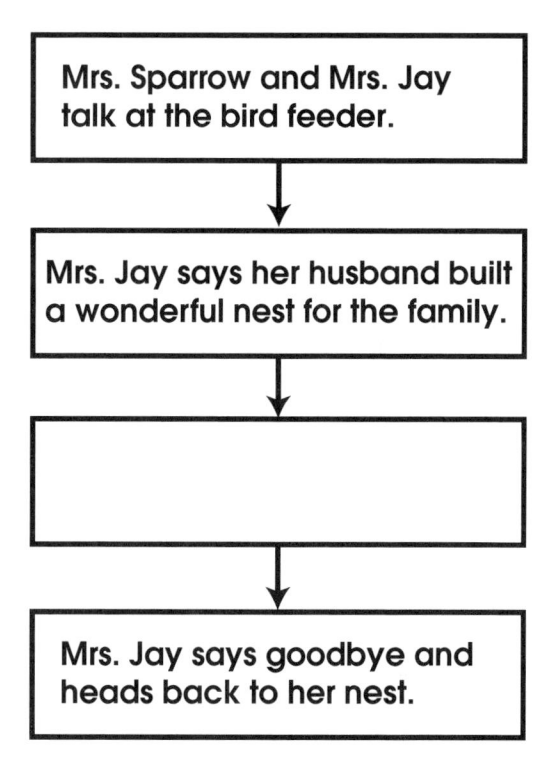

```
┌─────────────────────────────────┐
│ Mrs. Sparrow and Mrs. Jay       │
│ talk at the bird feeder.        │
└─────────────────────────────────┘
                │
                ▼
┌─────────────────────────────────┐
│ Mrs. Jay says her husband built │
│ a wonderful nest for the family.│
└─────────────────────────────────┘
                │
                ▼
┌─────────────────────────────────┐
│                                 │
└─────────────────────────────────┘
                │
                ▼
┌─────────────────────────────────┐
│ Mrs. Jay says goodbye and       │
│ heads back to her nest.         │
└─────────────────────────────────┘
```

Which of these belongs in the empty box?

○ A. Mrs. Jay lands at the bird feeder.

○ B. Mrs. Sparrow flies toward her home.

○ C. Mrs. Sparrow talks about the tiny nest the Hummingbirds built.

Reading

Use Pencil Please

35. What street do the birds live on?

   ○ A. Treeside Avenue

   ○ B. Birdhouse Drive

   ○ C. Feathertree Lane

36. List two things Mrs. Jay's husband used to build their new nest. Use information from the reading selection in your answer.

   a. _____

   _____

   b. _____

   _____

Go to next page

37. How are the Robin family and the Hummingbird family alike?

    ○   A. They make humming noises with their wings.

    ○   B. They aren't very friendly.

    ○   C. They have beautiful red feathers.

38. This sentence is from the selection.

    "It does look quite **cozy**."

    Which word is a synonym for **cozy**?

    ○   A. comfortable

    ○   B. ugly

    ○   C. hard

Reading

39. This sentence is from the selection.

    "They **don't** fly away when another bird comes by the feeder."

    What does the contraction **don't** mean?

    ○ A. do not
    ○ B. do nothing
    ○ C. do next

40. What kind of story is "Birds of a Feather"?

    ○ A. poem
    ○ B. nonfiction
    ○ C. fiction

Reading Practice Test 2

Reading R

Directions:

Today you will be taking a practice Reading assessment. This is a test of how well you understand what you read. The test consists of vocabulary questions and reading selections followed by questions about each reading selection. Three different types of questions appear on this test: multiple choice, short answer and extended response.

There are several important things to remember:

1. Read each reading selection carefully. You may look back at the reading selection as often as necessary. You may underline or mark parts of any selection.

2. Read each question carefully. Think about what is being asked. If a graph or other diagram goes with the question, look at it carefully to help you answer the question. Then choose or write the answer that you think is best.

3. When you write your answers, write them neatly and clearly in the space provided using a pencil.

4. When you answer a multiple choice question, make sure you fill in the circle next to the answer. Mark only one answer. If you do not know the answer to a question, skip it and go on. If you have time, go back to the questions you skipped and answer them before you hand in your Student Workbook.

6. If you finish the test early, you may check over your work. When you are finished and your Student Workbook has been collected, you may take out your silent work.

7. When you finish the test, you may not go on to, or look at the mathematics section of the Student Workbook.

Go to next page

Directions: Carefully read each question. Fill in the circle next to the correct answer.

1. The water pipe was **underground**.

   What kind of word is **underground**?

   ○ A. verb
   ○ B. compound
   ○ C. homonym

2. Which word is an antonym for **light**?

   ○ A. late
   ○ B. dark
   ○ C. right

Directions: Read the selection.

Carrots and Gravy

There are two foods I never want to see on my plate: carrots and gravy. I don't mean together. I don't like either of them. For as long as I can remember, I have never liked these two foods. I'm not sure why. Mom says I didn't even like them when I was little.

We have a rule in our house. At dinner, we have to try everything. I've tried carrots with salad. I've tried gravy with potatoes. Nothing works. I'm nine years old, and I still don't like carrots or gravy. I know I never will. Mom served carrots again last week. I knew I wouldn't like them. Mom just looked at me. I knew the rule. I swallowed the orange mess. I grabbed my throat. I grabbed my belly. I fell from my chair. Mom just watched me as I wiggled on the floor.

Reading

"Well, Julio, you've tried. No more carrots. No more gravy. I promise."

I had won the battle against carrots and gravy.

Mom kept her promise. Things were fine until a family dinner. Mom and I met my grandparents at their favorite place to eat. It was Grandpa's birthday. My uncle and his son, Jake, were there, too. Jake is a year older; he's in fourth grade. Jake and I both wanted hamburgers and French fries with lots of ketchup. We sat at the table, practicing our orders. A waitress came by and served us water.

"Your dinners will be here soon," she said.

"But we haven't ordered yet." Jake and I were confused.

"It's been taken care of," she said. "I just know you're going to love it."

My uncle had called ahead to save time. I was disappointed. I really wanted a hamburger.

The waitress was right. Our dinner started in no time at all. The salad came first. It was covered with little carrots. I tried to be polite. I pushed the carrots to the side of my plate. When my salad was free of carrots, I enjoyed every bite. "This isn't so bad," I thought.

The waitress took our salad plates. It was time for the main course. "Please!" I whispered to Jake, "Let it be something I like!" I held my breath. The plate was in front of me. I peeked. Turkey and mashed potatoes covered in gravy! Mom smiled at me. I didn't grab my throat or my belly. I gave Mom half a smile. I just moved things around on my plate during dinner. Everyone was busy talking. No one seemed to see.

"Are you going to eat that?" Jake asked. I shook my head no. He put my dinner onto his plate. "This is great!" I couldn't believe he thought so. All that gravy—yuck.

I thought Mom would be mad. But on our way home, she stopped at Happy Burger. I didn't even ask her to. "What will you have, Julio?" Mom asked.

"I'll take a cheeseburger and fries. No carrots. No gravy."

Reading

Directions: Use the selection to answer questions 3–9.

3. This paragraph is from the selection.

   "The waitress took our salad plates. It was time for the main course. "Please!" I whispered to Jake, "Let it be something I like!" I held my breath. The plate was in front of me. I peeked. Turkey and mashed potatoes covered in gravy! Mom smiled at me. I didn't grab my throat or my belly. I gave Mom half a smile. I just moved things around on my plate during dinner. Everyone was busy talking. No one seemed to see."

   What is the main idea of this paragraph?

   ○ A. Julio pretending to eat the dinner even though it is covered in gravy
   ○ B. Julio grabbing his belly and falling out of his chair
   ○ C. Jake taking Julio's dinner from him

4. What does Julio's mom decide about making Julio eat carrots?

   ○ A. Julio's mom decides Julio will have to eat carrots every night.
   ○ B. Julio's mom decides Julio will not have to eat any more carrots.
   ○ C. Julio's mom can't decide whether or not to make Julio eat carrots at dinner.

5. What does Julio do when he gets a salad with carrots on it?

   ○ A. Julio refuses to eat the salad.

   ○ B. Julio gives the salad to his cousin, Jake.

   ○ C. Julio pushes the carrots to the side; then, he eats the salad.

6. Read the first sentence of the summary below.

   Julio does not like carrots and gravy, and his mom tells him he will not have to eat them anymore.

   Which of the following completes the summary above?

   ○ A. Julio falls off his chair when he has to eat carrots. Julio's mom tells him he might still have to eat gravy.

   ○ B. Julio goes to a family dinner where carrots and gravy are served. Julio doesn't make a scene, so his mom takes him for a treat afterward.

   ○ C. Julio and his cousin Jake want to order hamburgers at dinner. The waitress brings a salad with carrots on it.

Go to next page

Reading

7. Look at the graphic organizer below.

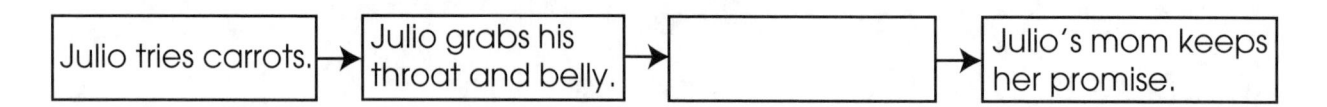

| Julio tries carrots. | → | Julio grabs his throat and belly. | → | | → | Julio's mom keeps her promise. |

Which of the following belongs in the empty box?

○ A. Julio's mom says he won't have to eat carrots anymore.

○ B. Julio is forced to eat carrots again.

○ C. Julio takes back his dinner plate after Jake steals it.

8. What do you think Julio will do in the future if he is served a dinner with carrots or gravy? Use information from the reading selection in your answer.

_____

_____

_____

_____

9. Where was Grandpa's birthday dinner held?

   ○ A. at a restaurant
   ○ B. at Happy Burger
   ○ C. at Grandpa's house

Reading

Directions: Read the selection.

Hiccup Man

Have you heard the story of Dan, The Hiccup Man? In third grade, Dan was the shortest kid in class. He couldn't reach the top library shelf or the coat rack. When he stood behind his classmates, he couldn't see anything. Dan wouldn't play basketball because he thought he was too short. But, as Dan left the school on the last day before summer vacation, there was something he didn't know. A few hiccups were about to change everything.

One hot, dry, summer day, Dan was on his way to dance class. He stopped to get a cold drink. He was very thirsty. He felt like he was going to dry up and blow away. Dan got a cold soda from a machine on the corner. He drank it so fast that he didn't even taste it. He stopped and looked at the can. That's when the hiccups started.

The hiccups weren't bad at first. In fact, it was his best dance class ever. The hiccups helped him jump higher. He could spin faster. Dan could even dance better. Everyone in the class wanted to know what he had done to dance better. Dan could only hiccup and smile. He didn't have an answer.

He put on his jeans and T-shirt after class. "That's strange," he thought to himself. "These jeans feel tight." He tied his shoes and started walking home. Dan hiccuped with every other step. By the time he got home, his jeans seemed four inches short. His T-shirt was too tight. He couldn't wait to change.

Dan's sides hurt from all his hiccuping. He tried everything he knew to make the hiccups stop. He held his breath. No hiccups . . . no hiccups . . . no . . . HI! That didn't work. He looked for someone to scare him. He found his brother in the kitchen. His brother started laughing. Dan's toes were sticking out of his shoes. Dan had grown too big for his clothes. With all his laughing, Dan's brother couldn't scare anyone. Dan tried a spoonful of sugar, but he hiccuped just as he got the spoon to his mouth. The sugar spilled all over the floor.

Dan's hiccups went on and on all summer. The more he hiccuped, the taller he grew. Dan worried the hiccups would never end. Then, one morning, they stopped. Something else happened, too. Dan stopped growing. Dan was very tired from all that hiccuping and growing. He slept for a week. He woke up in time for school to start.

Dan was excited. He was very tall now. On the first day of school, his friends did not recognize him. He was the tallest kid in school! When his teacher asked Dan what he had done over summer vacation, he smiled and said, "I hiccuped." The kids laughed and started calling him Dan, Dan, the Hiccup Man. Dan said he didn't mind, as long the hiccups never came back.

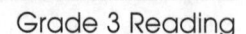

Reading

Directions: Use the selection to answer questions 10–21.

10. How does Dan feel about growing taller?

    ○ A. angry

    ○ B. unhappy

    ○ C. excited

11. How do Dan's feelings about the hiccups change?

    ○ A. At first, he thinks they are scary, but later, he decides they are fun.

    ○ B. At first, he thinks they are not so bad, but later, they make him worried.

    ○ C. At first, he thinks they are fun, but later, they make him angry.

12. These sentences are from the selection.

    "He was very thirsty. He felt like he was going to dry up and blow away."

    What made Dan so thirsty?

    ○ A. It was a hot summer day.
    ○ B. It was very windy outside.
    ○ C. Dan had been playing basketball.

13. This paragraph is from the selection.

    "The hiccups weren't bad at first. In fact, it was his best dance class ever. The hiccups helped him jump higher. He could spin faster. Dan could even dance better. Everyone in the class wanted to know what he had done to dance better. Dan could only hiccup and smile. He didn't have an answer."

    How do the hiccups help Dan in this paragraph?

    ○ A. Dan is at school, and the hiccups help him reach the coat rack.
    ○ B. Dan is playing basketball, and the hiccups help him jump higher.
    ○ C. Dan is at dance class, and the hiccups help him dance better.

Reading

14. What is Dan's problem?

    ○ A. Dan's classmates call him the Hiccup Man.

    ○ B. Dan is the worst dancer in his class.

    ○ C. Dan can't stop hiccuping.

15. How is Dan's problem solved?

    ○ A. Dan takes a special medicine.

    ○ B. No solution is given.

    ○ C. Dan goes to the doctor.

16. List two things that the hiccups help Dan to do in dance class. Use information from the reading selection in your answer.

    a. _____

    _____

    b. _____

    _____

Go to next page

17. How long did Dan sleep once the hiccups stopped?

    ○ A. a day
    ○ B. a week
    ○ C. a year

18. This sentence is from the selection.

    "Dan worried the hiccups would **never** end."

    Which word or words are a synonym for **never**?

    ○ A. not ever
    ○ B. definitely
    ○ C. soon

Reading

19. Which of the following choices best completes the chart below?

Things that happened because Dan grew quickly:
• jeans got four inches shorter
• toes stuck out from his shoes
•

- ○ A. sugar spilled on the floor
- ○ B. hiccups lasted all summer
- ○ C. T-shirt became too tight

20. What is this selection about?

   _____

   _____

   List three details that support the main idea.

   a. _____

      _____

   b. _____

      _____

   c. _____

      _____

Reading

21. What is the purpose of this story?

　　○　A. to teach the reader how to be a good dancer

　　○　B. to tell the reader how to get rid of the hiccups

　　○　C. to entertain the reader with a fun story

Directions: Read the selection.

Journal Writing

Writing in a journal is a great way to remember things in your life. Writers use journals to write their thoughts and ideas. Some people use journals to remember story ideas. Others write about bad days or happy times. A journal can help you think about what is happening in your life. When you read what you have written in your journal, you can learn from your daily life. A journal can also be called a diary.

It doesn't take fancy things to start a journal. You can start with a notebook and a pen or a pencil. You can also use a computer to start your journal. The important thing is to write your thoughts and ideas. You can write them on paper. You can also type them. Do what is best for you.

Try to write in your journal every day. You don't need to write for a long time. You may only write for five or ten minutes at first. You may find that you want to write for a few more minutes once you get started. Writing in a journal is a good way to learn how to write better. Even though your journal is filled with your own words, try to use your best handwriting (if you're writing in a notebook). You want to be able to read what you have written! Also, try to spell words correctly and use sentences. Working on these things will help you become a better writer.

Another secret to journal writing is to keep track of your writing. Put the date on each journal page. If you date your journal pages, you will remember when things happened. Every week or so, go back and read what you have written. You might find that you have forgotten something that once seemed important. You might also find words that surprise you. No matter what, keep writing. You may be surprised at how much you have to say.

Reading

Directions: Use the selection to answer questions 22–31.

22. According to the author, what is the effect of putting a date on each of your journal pages?

    ○ A. You will remember when things happened.

    ○ B. You will become a better writer.

    ○ C. You will get better grades in school.

23. Read the headlines of these newspaper articles:

    Headline 1: Journal Writers Are Not Better Writers

    Headline 2: Keeping a Journal Helps Students Learn

    Headline 3: Fancy Journals Are Better to Write In

    Which headline would the author most likely agree with?

    ○ A. Headline 1

    ○ B. Headline 2

    ○ C. Headline 3

Reading

24. This sentence is from the selection.

    "Writing in a journal is a good way to learn how to write better."

    Which word lets you know this is an opinion?

    - ○ A. way
    - ○ B. good
    - ○ C. learn

25. Which sentence from the selection is not an opinion?

    - ○ A. Writing in a journal is a great way to remember things in your life.
    - ○ B. You want to be able to read what you have written!
    - ○ C. A journal can also be called a diary.

26. This sentence is from the selection.

    "Even though your journal is **filled** with your own words, try to use your best handwriting (if you're writing in a notebook)."

    What is another way to say **filled**?

    - ○ A. full of
    - ○ B. emptied out
    - ○ C. dressed up

Reading

27. Fill in the web with ideas from the selection about how to use a journal.

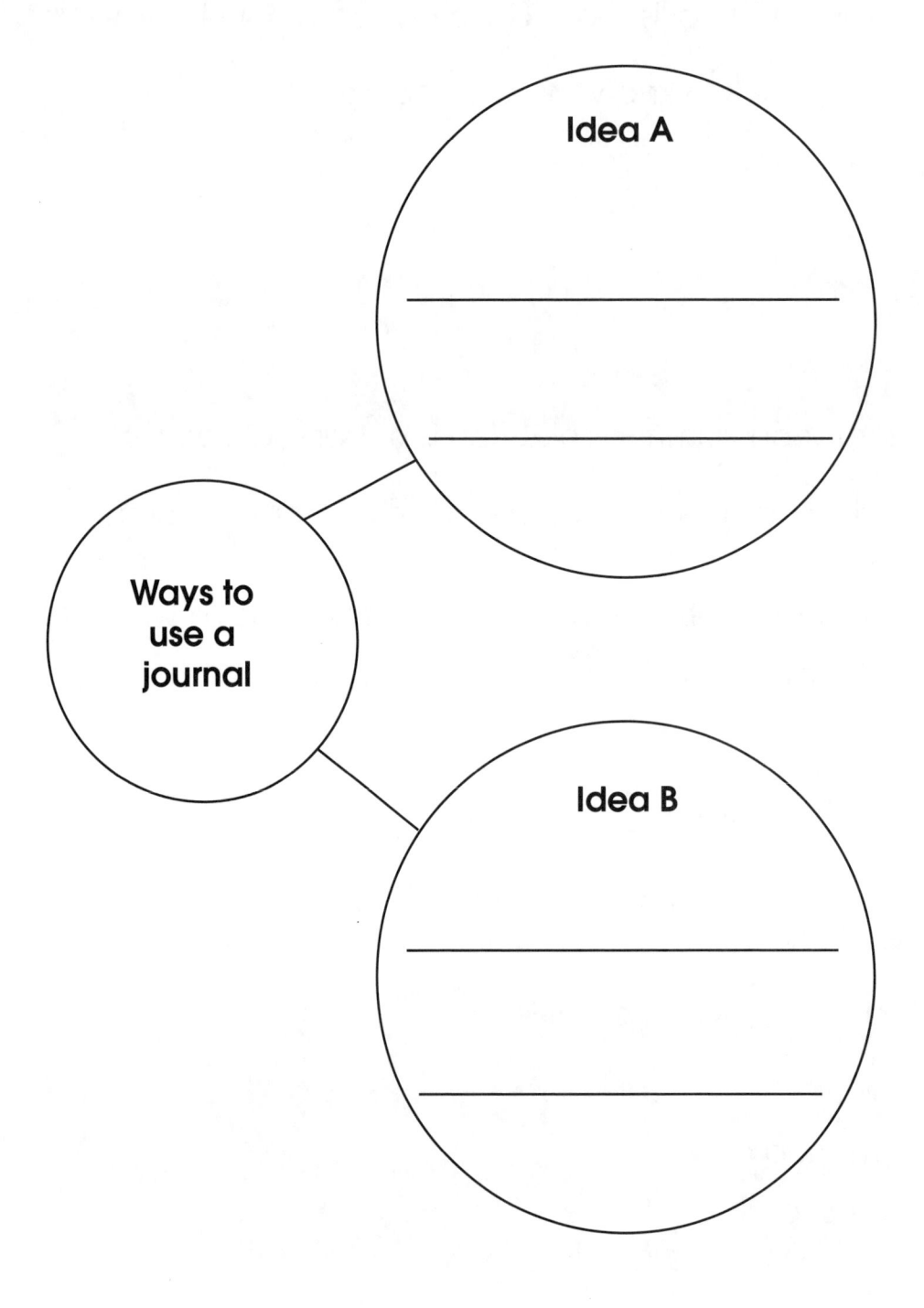

Idea A
_____
_____

Ways to use a journal

Idea B
_____
_____

28. List two things you need if you want to keep a journal. Use information from the reading selection in your answer.

a. _____

_____

b. _____

_____

29. According to the author, how often should you write in your journal?

○ A. daily

○ B. once a month

○ C. once a year

Reading — **Use Pencil Please**

30. List two ways writing in a journal can help you become a better writer. Use information from the reading selection in your answer.

   a. _____

   b. _____

31. Which of the following is not something to do when keeping a journal?

   ○ A. date each journal page

   ○ B. try to write in your journal every day

   ○ C. stop writing when you are out of ideas

Go to next page

Directions: Read the selection.

Penguins

Penguins are very interesting animals. They are members of the bird family. They lay eggs, have feathers, and are **warmblooded**. Unlike most birds, penguins do not fly. Instead of having wings on its body, a penguin has long, flat flippers that help it swim underwater for food.

There are 17 different kinds of penguins. Penguins can be found only in the Southern Hemisphere. Some penguins live on hot, tropical islands, while others live in very cold, icy areas such as Antarctica. Most penguins spend three-quarters of their time in the water.

Penguins don't look like other birds. A penguin has a long head, a short neck, a long body, and a short tail. A penguin's two legs and webbed feet (like a duck's feet) are set far back on its body, which helps it to stand upright on land.

Penguins move around on land by walking, jumping, or sliding. Penguins living on icy land move around by sliding down hills and slopes on their bellies. Other kinds of penguins waddle, using a swinging back-and-forth motion when they walk. Some penguins get around by hopping or jumping.

All penguins are similar in color. Penguins have white bellies and black backs. The colors are a kind of protection against **predators**. When a penguin is in the water floating on its belly, a predator, such as a killer whale or leopard seal, cannot see the penguin. This is because when the predator looks up through the water, the light shining through the water looks white, just like the penguin's belly. As the penguin floats in the water, its back and head on the top of the water are also hard to see because the penguin blends in with the dark color of the water.

Word Bank
warmblooded—able to keep a steady body temperature, despite surrounding air temperatures **predators**—animals that hunt, kill, and eat other animals

Go to next page

Directions: Use the selection to answer questions 32-40.

32. This paragraph is from the selection.

    "Penguins are very interesting animals. They are members of the bird family. They lay eggs, have feathers, and are warmblooded. Unlike most birds, penguins do not fly. Instead of having wings on its body, a penguin has long, flat flippers that help it swim underwater for food."

    What is the main idea of this paragraph?

    - A. Penguins have flippers.
    - B. Penguins are interesting animals.
    - C. Penguins lay eggs.

33. Which word means an animal that hunts, kills, and eats other animals?

    - A. emperor
    - B. molt
    - C. predator

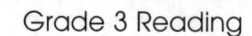

Reading

34. Which sentence from the selection is an opinion?

    ○ A. There are 17 different kinds of penguins.

    ○ B. Penguins are very interesting animals.

    ○ C. A penguin has a long head, a short neck, a long body, and a short tail.

35. This sentence is from the selection.

    "**Unlike** most birds, penguins do not fly."

    What is the prefix of **unlike**?

    ○ A. un-

    ○ B. -like

    ○ C. -ke

36. List four ways penguins move around on land. Use information from the reading selection in your answer.

a. _____

_____

b. _____

_____

c. _____

_____

d. _____

_____

37. What kind of selection is "Penguins"?

   ○ A. nonfiction

   ○ B. fairy tale

   ○ C. poem

Reading

38. How do penguins protect themselves from predators?

   ○ A. They run into igloos they have built.

   ○ B. Their natural coloring makes them hard to see.

   ○ C. They hide in underwater caves.

39. How many kinds of penguins are there?

_____

In what part of the world can you find penguins?

_____

What kinds of climates do penguins live in?

_____

_____

Reading

40. Which answer best completes the chart?

Penguin Characteristics
• bird family
• lay eggs
• have feathers
•

- A. have wings
- B. can fly
- C. warmblooded

Mathematics

Introduction

In the Mathematics section of Ohio's state assessment, you will be asked questions to test what you have learned so far in school. These questions are based on the mathematical skills you have been taught in school through third grade. The questions you will answer are not meant to confuse or trick you, but are written so you have the best chance to show what you know.

Questions I Will Answer on the Ohio's State Assessment

You will answer multiple-choice, short-answer, and extended-response questions on the Mathematics assessment. Multiple-choice items have three answer choices, and only one is correct. Short-answer items require you to write a number, phrase, sentence, or number sentence and show work. Extended-response items require you to write one or more number sentences, solve multistep problems, show work, and/or explain your answer by writing a few phrases or a complete sentence or two.

Examples of a multiple-choice item, a short-answer item, and an extended-response item are shown below and on the following pages.

1. William's basketball team is having a pizza party. There are eight players on the team. Three pizzas with eight slices each have been ordered. Each player will get an equal amount of pizza.

   Which picture shows how much pizza each player will get?

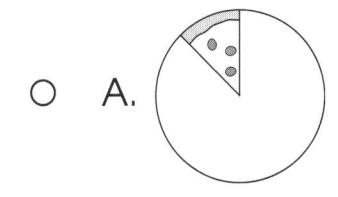

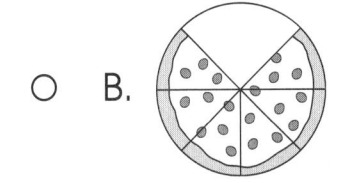

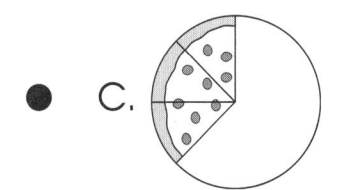

   ○ A.

   ○ B.

   ● C.

2. Write the missing numbers to continue this pattern.

   4, 7, 10, 13, __16__, __19__

   Describe the rule for this pattern.

   The rule is to add 3.

3. The lunch menu for Ana Banana's Snack Shack is shown.

Ana Banana's Snack Shack Lunch Menu

Peanut Butter and Jelly Sandwich $3.50

Lemonade $1.00

Ice Cream Cone $2.65

Kara has $5.00.

What is the most items Kara can purchase from the menu? __2__

Show how you found your answer using pictures, words or numbers.

```
1 peanut butter and jelly sandwich: $3.50
                     1 lemonade: + $1.00
                                 ───────
                                 = $4.50

                                   $5.00
                                 − $4.50
                                 ───────
                                 = $.50
```

Lindsey purchased two items for $3.65.

Show how Lindsey could have purchased these items.

1 ice cream cone: $2.65
1 lemonade: + $1.00
———
= $3.65

Item Distribution on Ohio's State Assessment for Grade 3 Mathematics

Number of Items	40
Number of Multiple-Choice Questions	32
Number of Short-Answer Questions	6
Number of Extended-Response Questions	2

Scoring

Ohio's state assessment for Grade 3 Mathematics includes three types of test items: multiple choice, short answer, and extended response. The Mathematics test includes 32 multiple-choice items, six short-answer items, and two extended-response items.

Multiple-Choice Items

Multiple-choice items require you to select the correct answer from a list of three choices. Each multiple-choice item is worth one point.

Short-Answer and Extended-Response Items

On the Mathematics assessment, item-specific rubrics are used for each constructed-response question (short answer or extended response). Conventions of writing (sentence structure, word choice, usage, grammar, spelling, and mechanics) will not affect the scoring of short-answer and extended-response items unless there is interference with the clear communication of ideas.

Short-Answer Scoring

Short-answer items require a brief written response. Student responses receive a score of 0, 1 or 2 points. Each short-answer item has an item-specific scoring guideline. These written responses may require supporting work or explanations. The following general two-point scoring guideline for short-answer items is used as a template to develop item-specific scoring guidelines for each individual short-answer item.

A **2-point response** provides a complete interpretation and/or correct solution. It demonstrates a thorough understanding of the concept or task. It indicates logical reasoning and conclusions. It is accurate, relevant, and complete.

A **1-point response** provides evidence of a partial interpretation and/or solution process. It demonstrates an incomplete understanding of the concept or task. It contains minor flaws in reasoning. It neglects to address some aspect of the task.

A **Zero-point response** does not meet the criteria required to earn one point. The response indicates inadequate understanding of the task and/or the idea or concept needed to answer the item. It may only repeat information given in the test item. The response may provide an incorrect solution/response and the provided supportive information may be totally irrelevant to the item, or possibly, no other information is shown. The student may have written on a different topic or written "I don't know."

Extended-Response Scoring

Extended-response items require students to demonstrate understanding in depth. Student responses receive a score of 0, 1, 2, 3 or 4 points. Each extended-response item has an item-specific scoring guideline. These written responses may include explanations, appropriate charts, tables, graphs, or other graphic organizers. The following general four-point rubric for extended-response items is used as a template to develop item-specific scoring guidelines for each individual extended-response item.

A **4-point response** provides essential aspects of a complete interpretation and/or a correct solution. The response thoroughly addresses the points relevant to the concept or task. It provides strong evidence that information reasoning, and conclusions have a definite logical relationship. It is clearly focused and organized, showing relevance to the concept, task and/or solution process.

A **3-point response** provides essential elements of an interpretation and/or a solution. It addresses the points relevant to the concept or task. It provides ample evidence that information, reasoning, and conclusions have a logical relationship. It is focused and organized, showing relevance to the concept, task, or solution process.

A **2-point response** provides a partial interpretation and/or solution. It somewhat addresses the points relevant to the concept or task. It provides some evidence that information, reasoning, and conclusions have a relationship. It is relevant to the concept and/or task, but there are gaps in focus and organization.

A **1-point response** provides an unclear, inaccurate interpretation and/or solution. It fails to address or omits significant aspects of the concept or task. It provides unrelated or unclear evidence that information, reasoning, and conclusions have a relationship. There is little evidence of focus or organization relevant to the concept, task and/or solution process.

A **Zero-point response** does not meet the criteria required to earn one point. The response indicates inadequate understanding of the task and/or the idea or concept needed to answer the item. It may only repeat information given in the test item. The response may provide an incorrect solution/response and the provided supportive information may be totally irrelevant to the item, or possibly, no other information is shown. The student may have written on a different topic or written "I don't know."

Glossary

addend: Numbers added together to give a sum. For example, 2 + 7 = 9. The numbers 2 and 7 are addends.

addition: An operation joining two or more sets where the result is the whole.

A.M.: The hours from midnight to noon; from Latin words *ante meridiem* meaning before noon.

analyze: To break down information into parts so that it may be more easily understood.

angle: A figure formed by two rays that meet at the same end point called a vertex. Angles can be obtuse, acute, right, or straight.

area: The number of square units needed to cover a region. The most common abbreviation for area is A.

Associative Property of Addition: The grouping of addends can be changed and the sum will be the same. Example: (3 + 1) + 2 = 6; 3 + (1 + 2) = 6.

Associative Property of Multiplication: The grouping of factors can be changed and the product will be the same. Example: (3 x 2) x 4 = 24; 3 x (2 x 4) = 24.

attribute: A characteristic or distinctive feature.

average: A number found by adding two or more quantities together and then dividing the sum by the number of quantities. For example, in the set {9, 5, 4}, the average is 6: 9 + 5 + 4 = 18; 18 ÷ 3 = 6. *See mean.*

axes: Plural of axis. Perpendicular lines used as reference lines in a coordinate system or graph; traditionally, the horizontal axis (*x*-axis) represents the independent variable and the vertical axis (*y*-axis) represents the dependent variable.

bar graph: A graph using bars to show data.

capacity: The amount an object holds when filled.

chart: A way to show information such as in a graph or table.

circle: Closed, curved line made up of points that are all the same distance from a point inside called the center.
Example: A circle with center point P is shown below.

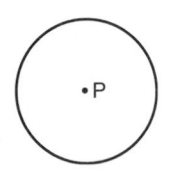

circle graph: Sometimes called a pie chart; a way of representing data that shows the fractional part or percentage of an overall set as an appropriately-sized wedge of a circle.
Example:

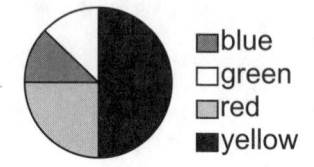

■ blue
□ green
▨ red
■ yellow

circumference: The boundary line or perimeter of a circle; also, the length of the perimeter of a circle. Example:

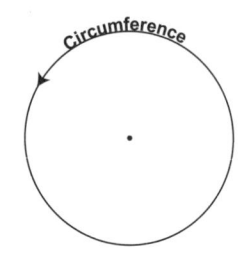

Commutative Property of Addition: Numbers can be added in any order and the sum will be the same. Example: 3 + 4 = 4 + 3.

Commutative Property of Multiplication: Numbers can be multiplied in any order and the product will be the same. Example: 3 x 6 = 6 x 3.

compare: To look for similarities and differences. For example, is one number greater than, less than, or equal to another number?

conclusion: A statement that follows logically from other facts.

Glossary

cone: A solid figure with a circle as its base and a curved surface that meets at a point called a vertex.

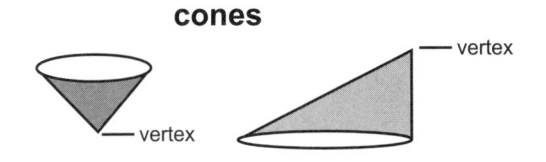

cones

congruent figures: Figures that have the same shape and size.

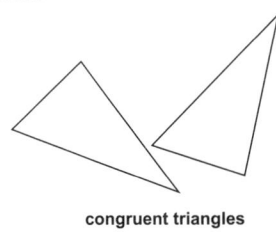

congruent triangles

cube: A solid figure with six faces that are congruent (equal) squares.

cylinder: A solid figure with two circular bases that are congruent (equal) and parallel to each other connected by a curved lateral surface.

data: Information that is collected.

decimal number: A number expressed in base 10, such as 39,456 where each digit's value is determined by multiplying it by some power of ten.

denominator: The bottom number in a fraction.

diagram: A drawing that represents a mathematical situation.

difference: The answer when subtracting two numbers.

distance: The space between two points.

dividend: A number in a division problem that is divided. Dividend ÷ divisor = quotient. Example: In 15 ÷ 3 = 5, 15 is the dividend.

$$\text{divisor}\overline{)\text{dividend}}^{\text{quotient}} \qquad 3\overline{)15}^{\,5}$$

divisible: Can be divided by another number without leaving a remainder. Example: 12 is divisible by 3 because 12 ÷ 3 is an integer, namely 4.

division: An operation that tells how many equal groups there are or how many are in each group.

divisor: The number by which another number is divided. Example: In 15 ÷ 3 = 5, 3 is the divisor.

$$\text{divisor}\overline{)\text{dividend}}^{\text{quotient}} \qquad 3\overline{)15}^{\,5}$$

edge: The line segment where two faces of a solid figure meet.

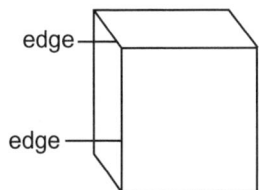

equivalent fractions: Two fractions with equal values.

equality: Two or more sets of values that are equal.

equation: A number sentence that says two expressions are equal (=).
Example: 4 + 8 = 6 + 6.

estimate: To find an approximate value or measurement of something without exact calculation.

even number: A whole number that has a 0, 2, 4, 6, or 8 in the ones place. A number that is a multiple of 2. Examples: 0, 4, and 678 are even numbers.

Glossary

expanded form: A number written as the sum of the values of its digits.
Example: 546 = 500 + 40 + 6.

expression: A combination of variables, numbers, and symbols that represent a mathematical relationship.

face: The sides of a solid figure. For example, a cube has six faces that are all squares. The pyramid below has five faces—four triangles and one square.

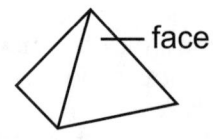

factor: One of two or more numbers that are multiplied together to give a product. Example: In 4 x 3 = 12, 4, and 3 are factors of 12.

fact family: A group of related facts using the same numbers. Example: 5 + 8 = 13; 13 − 8 = 5.

figure: A geometric figure is a set of points and/or lines in 2 or 3 dimensions.

flip: (reflection) The change in a position of a figure that is the result of picking it up and turning it over. Example: Reversing a "b" to a "d". Tipping a "p" to a "b" or a "b" to a "p" as shown below:

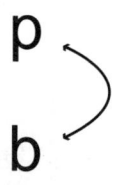

fraction: A symbol, such as 2/8 or 5/3, used to name a part of a whole, a part of a set, or a location on the number line. Examples:

$$\frac{\text{numerator}}{\text{denominator}} = \frac{\text{dividend}}{\text{divisor}} =$$

$$\frac{\text{\# of parts under consideration}}{\text{\# of parts in a set}}$$

function machine: Applies a function rule to a set of numbers, which determines a corresponding set of numbers.
Example: Input 9 → Rule x 7 → Output 63. If you apply the function rule "multiply by 7" to the values 5, 7, and 9, the corresponding values are:
5 → 35
7 → 49
9 → 63

graph: A "picture" showing how certain facts are related to each other or how they compare to one another. Some examples of types of graphs are line graphs, pie charts, bar graphs, scatterplots, and pictographs.

grid: A pattern of regularly-spaced horizontal and vertical lines on a plane that can be used to locate points and graph equations.

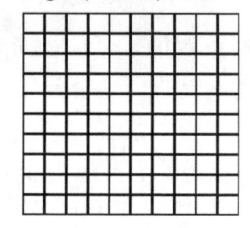

hexagon: A six-sided polygon. The total measure of the angles within a hexagon is 720°.

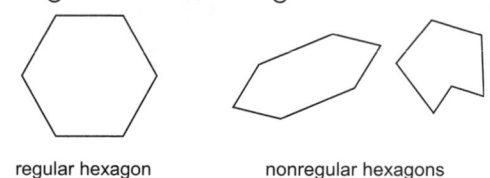

regular hexagon   nonregular hexagons

impossible event: An event that can never happen. It's probability is represented mathematically as 0.

integer: Any number, positive or negative, that is a whole number distance away from zero on a number line, in addition to zero. Specifically, an integer is any number in the set {. . .-3,-2,-1, 0, 1, 2, 3. . .}. Examples of integers include 1, 5, 273, -2, -35, and -1,375.

110 Student Workbook

Glossary

intersecting lines: Lines that cross at a point. Examples:

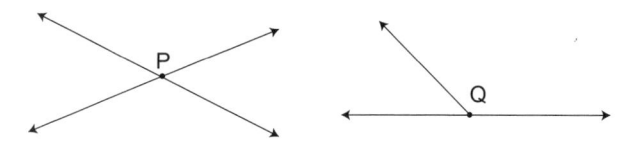

isosceles triangle: A triangle with at least two sides the same length.

justify: To prove or show how something is true using logic and evidence.

key: An explanation of what each symbol represents in a pictograph.

kilometer (kg): A metric unit of length. 1 kilometer = 1,000 meters.

line: A straight path of points that goes on forever in both directions.

line graph: A graph that uses a line or a curve to show how data changes over time.

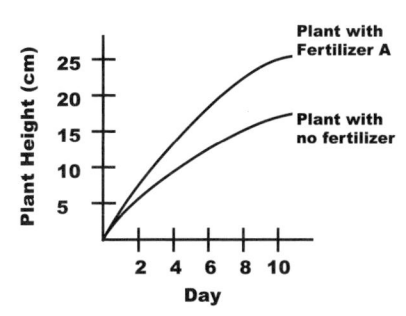

line of symmetry: A line on which a figure can be folded into two parts so that the parts match exactly.

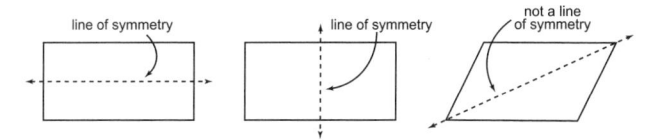

liter (L): A metric unit of capacity usually used for liquids. 1 liter = 1,000 milliliters.

mass: The amount of matter an object has.

mean: Also called arithmetic average. A number found by adding two or more quantities together; and then dividing the sum by the number of quantities. For example, in the set {9, 5, 4} the mean is 6: 9 + 5 + 4 = 18; 18 ÷ 3 = 6. *See average.*

median: The middle number when numbers are put in order from least to greatest or from greatest to least. For example, in the set of numbers 6, 7, 8, 9, 10, the number 8 is the median (middle) number.

meter (m): A metric unit of length. 1 meter = 100 centimeters.

method: A systematic way of accomplishing a task.

mixed number: A number consisting of a whole number and a fraction.
Example: $6\frac{2}{3}$.

mode: The number or numbers that occurs most often in a set of data. Example: The mode of {1, 3, 4, 5, 5, 7, 9} is 5.

multiple: A product of a number and any other whole number.
Examples: {2, 4, 6, 8, 10, 12,…} are multiples of 2.

multiplication: An operation on two numbers that tells how many in all. The first number is the number of sets and the second number tells how many in each set.

number line: A line that shows numbers in order using a scale. Equal intervals are marked and usually labeled on the number line.

number sentence: An expression of a relationship between quantities as an equation or an inequality. Examples: 7 + 7 = 8 + 6; 14 < 92; 56 + 4 > 59.

numerator: The top number in a fraction.

Glossary

octagon: An eight-sided polygon. The total measure of the angles within an octagon is 1080°.

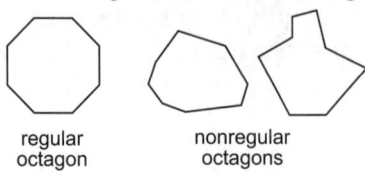

regular octagon   nonregular octagons

odd number: A whole number that has 1, 3, 5, 7, or 9 in the ones place. An odd number is not divisible by 2. Examples: The numbers 53 and 701 are odd numbers.

operation: A mathematical process that combines numbers; basic operations of arithmetic include addition, subtraction, multiplication, and division.

order: To arrange numbers from the least to greatest or from the greatest to least.

ordered pair: Two numbers inside a set of parentheses separated by a comma that are used to name a point on a coordinate grid.

parallelogram: A quadrilateral in which opposite sides are parallel.

parallel lines: Lines in the same plane that never intersect.

pattern: An organized and predictable arrangement of numbers, pictures, etc. Examples: 3, 6, 9, 12 or ® 0 ® 0 ® 0.

pentagon: A five-sided polygon. The total measure of the angles within a pentagon is 540°.

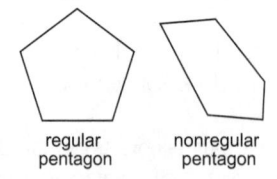

regular pentagon   nonregular pentagon

perimeter: The distance around a figure.

perpendicular lines: Two lines that intersect to form a right angle (90 degrees).

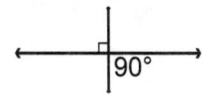

pictograph: A graph that uses pictures or symbols to represent similar data. The value of each picture is interpreted by a "key" or "legend."

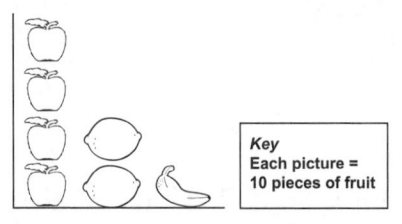

Key
Each picture = 10 pieces of fruit

place value: The value given to the place a digit has in a number.
Example: In the number 135, the 1 is in the hundreds place so it represents 100 (1 x 100), the 3 is in the tens place so it represents 30 (3 x 10), and the 5 is in the ones place so it represents 5 (5 x 1).

P.M.: The hours from noon to midnight; from the Latin words *post meridiem* meaning after noon.

point: An exact position often marked by a dot.

polygon: A closed figure made up of straight line segments.

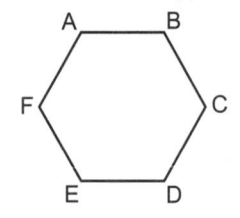

ABCDEF is a polygon.

possible event: An event that might or might not happen.

predict: To tell what you believe may happen in the future.

prediction: A prediction is a description of what may happen before it happens.

probability: The likelihood that something will happen.

product: The answer to a multiplication problem. Example: In 3 x 4 = 12, 12 is the product.

Glossary

pyramid: A solid figure in which the base is a polygon and the faces are triangles with a common point called a vertex.

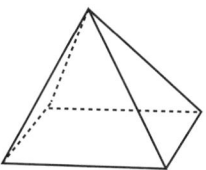

quadrilateral: A four-sided polygon. Rectangles, squares, parallelograms, rhombi, and trapezoids are all quadrilaterals. The total measure of the angles within a quadrilateral is 360°. Example: ABCD is a quadrilateral.

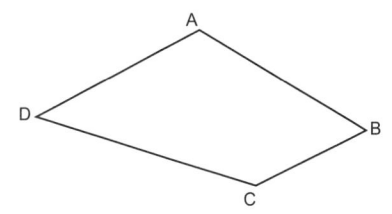

questionnaire: A set of questions for a survey.

quotient: The answer in a division problem. Dividend ÷ divisor = quotient.
Example: In 15 ÷ 3 = 5, 5 is the quotient.

range: The difference between the largest number and the smallest number in a data set. For example, in the set {4, 7, 10, 12, 36, 7, 2}, the range is 34. The largest number (36) minus the smallest number (2): (36 – 2 = 34).

rectangle: A quadrilateral with four right angles. A square is one example of a rectangle.

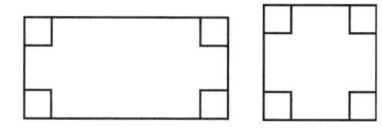

reflection: The change in the position of a figure that is the result of picking it up and turning it over. *See flip.*

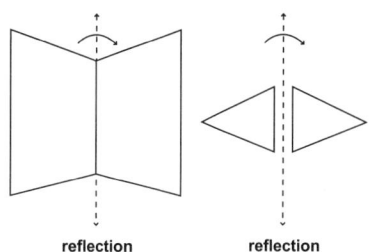

represent: To present clearly; describe; show.

remainder: The number that is left over after dividing. Example: In 31 ÷ 7 = 4 R 3 the 3 is the remainder.

rhombus: A quadrilateral with opposite sides parallel and all sides the same length. A square is one kind of rhombus.

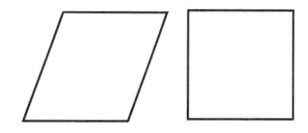

right angle: An angle that forms a square corner and measures 90 degrees.

right triangle: A triangle having one right angle. *See angle and triangle.*

rounding: Replacing a number with another number that tells about how much or how many to the nearest ten, hundred, thousand, and so on. Example: 52 rounded to the nearest 10 is 50.

Glossary

rule: A way of describing the relationship between two sets of numbers. Example: In the following data, the rule is to add 3:

Input	Output
3	6
5	8
9	12

ruler: A straight-edged instrument used for measuring the lengths of objects. A ruler usually measures smaller units of length, such as inches or centimeters.

scale: The numbers that show the units used on a graph.

sequence: A set of numbers arranged in a special order or pattern.

set: A group made up of numbers, figures, or parts.

side: A line segment connected to other segments to form the boundary of a polygon.

similar: A description for figures that have the same shape.

slide (translation): The change in the position of a figure that moves up, down, or sideways. Example: scooting a book on a table.

solids: Figures in three dimensions.

solve: To find the solution to an equation or problem; finding the values of unknown variables that will make a true mathematical statement.

sphere: A solid figure in the shape of a ball. Example: a basketball is a sphere.

square: A rectangle with congruent (equal) sides. *See rectangle.*

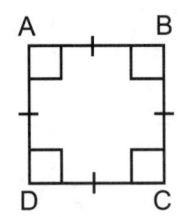

square number: The product of a number multiplied by itself. Example: 49 is a square number (7 x 7 = 49).

square unit: The square with sides 1 unit long, used to measure area.

standard form: A way to write a number showing only its digits. Example: 2,389.

standard units of measure: Units of measure commonly used; generally classified in the U.S. as the customary system or the metric system:

Customary System:
Length
1 foot (ft) = 12 inches (in)
1 yard (yd) = 3 feet or 36 inches
1 mile (mi) = 1,760 yards or 5,280 feet

Weight
16 ounces (oz) = 1 pound (lb)
2,000 pounds = 1 ton (t)

Capacity
1 pint (pt) = 2 cups (c)
1 quart (qt) = 2 pints
1 gallon (gal) = 4 quarts

Metric System:
Length
1 centimeter (cm) = 10 millimeters (mm)
1 decimeter (dm) = 10 centimeters
1 meter (m) = 100 centimeters
1 kilometer (km) = 1,000 meters

Weight
1,000 milligrams (mg) = 1 gram (g)
1,000 grams (g) = 1 kilogram (kg)

Capacity
1 liter (l) = 1,000 milliliters (ml)

Glossary

strategy: A plan used in problem solving, such as looking for a pattern, drawing a diagram, working backward, etc.

subtraction: The operation that finds the difference between two numbers.

sum: The answer when adding two or more addends. Addend + Addend = Sum.

summary: A series of statements containing evidence, facts, and/or procedures that support a result.

survey: A way to collect data by asking a certain number of people the same question and recording their answers.

symmetry: A figure has symmetry if it can be folded along a line so that both parts match exactly.

table: A method of displaying data in rows and columns.

temperature: A measure of hot or cold in degrees.

translation: A change in the position of a figure that moves it up, down, or sideways. *See slide.*

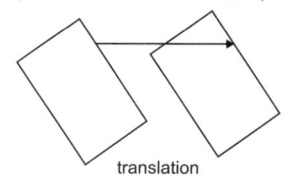

translation

triangle: A polygon with three sides. The sum of the angles of a triangle is always equal to 180°.

turn: The change in the position of a figure that moves it around a point. Also called a rotation. Example: The hands of a clock turn around the center of the clock in a clockwise direction.

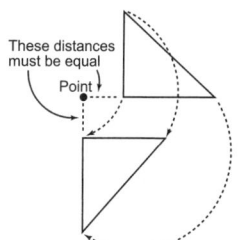

These distances must be equal
Point

unlikely event: An event that probably will not happen.

vertex: The point where two rays meet to form an angle or where the sides of a polygon meet or the point where 3 or more edges meet in a solid figure.

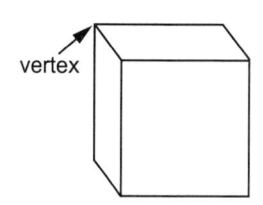

vertex

whole number: An integer in the set {0, 1, 2, 3 . . .}. In other words, a whole number is any number used when counting in addition to zero.

word forms: The number written in words. Examples: 546 is "five hundred forty-six." The "<" symbol means "is less than." The ">" symbol means "is greater than." The "=" symbol means "equals" or "is equal to."

Examples of Common Two-Dimensional Geometric Shapes

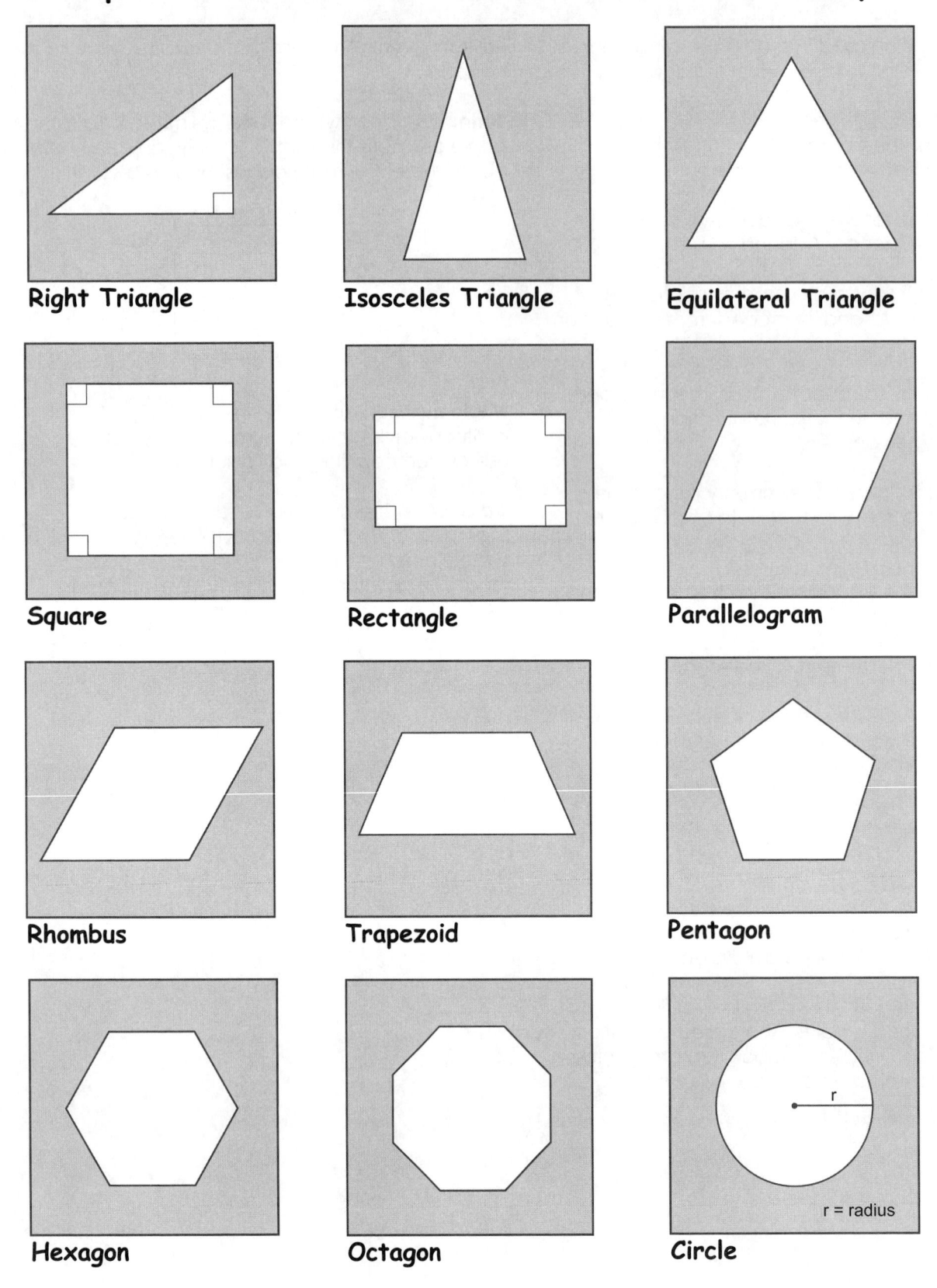

Right Triangle

Isosceles Triangle

Equilateral Triangle

Square

Rectangle

Parallelogram

Rhombus

Trapezoid

Pentagon

Hexagon

Octagon

Circle

r = radius

Examples of How Lines Interact

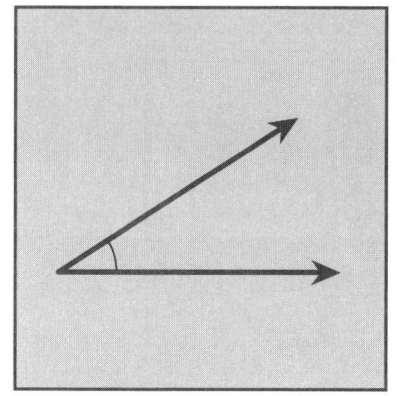

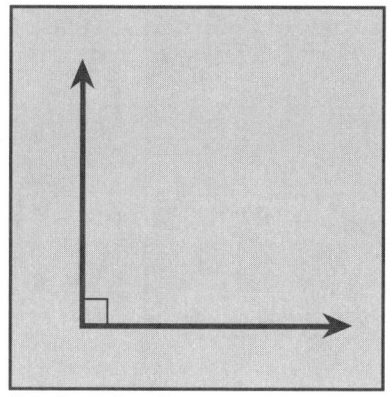

Acute Angle

Right Angle

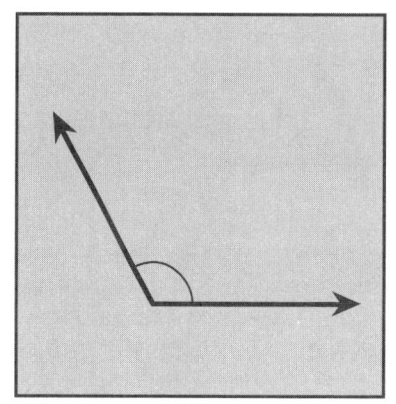

Obtuse Angle

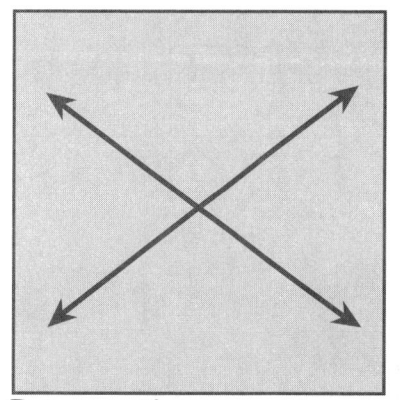

Intersecting

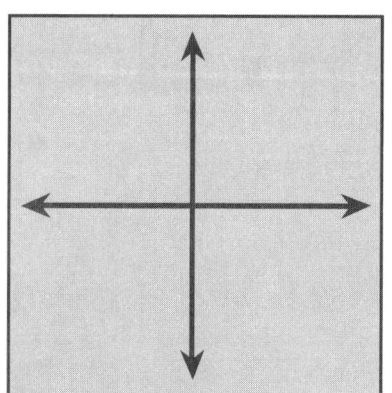

Perpendicular

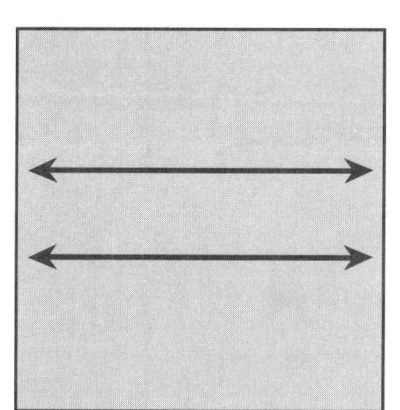

Parallel

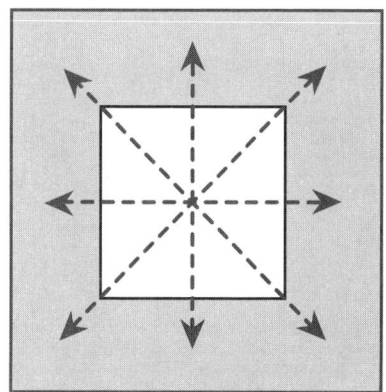

Lines of Symmetry

Examples of Common Types of Graphs

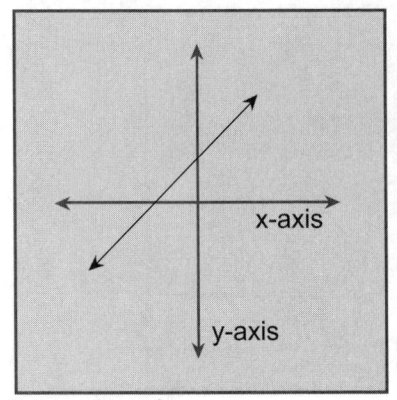

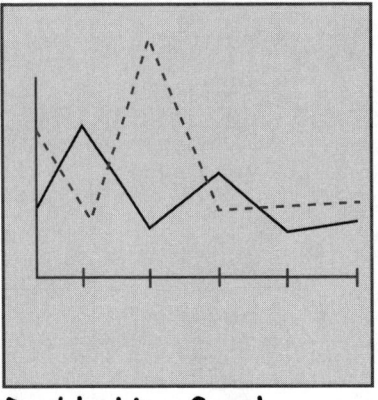

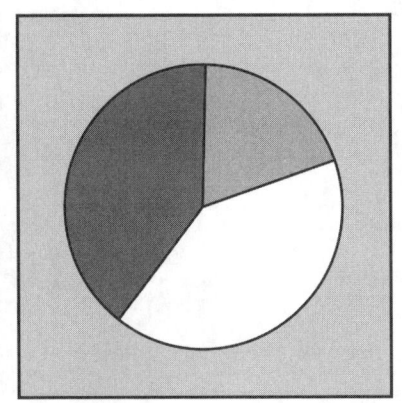

Line Graph

Double Line Graph

Pie Chart

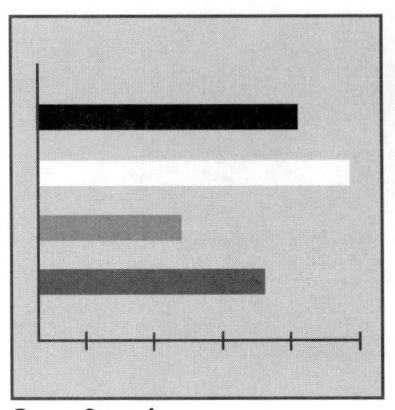

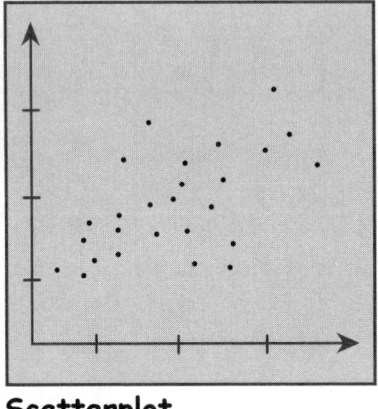

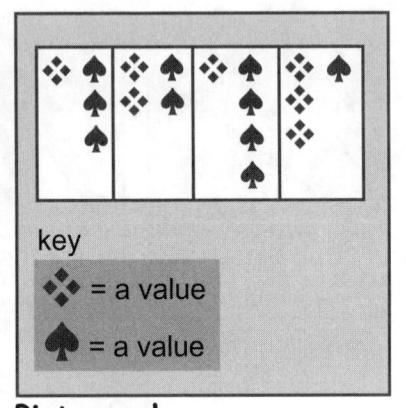

Bar Graph

Scatterplot

Pictograph

key
♦ = a value
♠ = a value

Examples of Common Three-Dimensional Objects

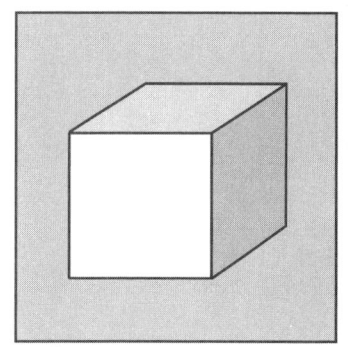

Cube

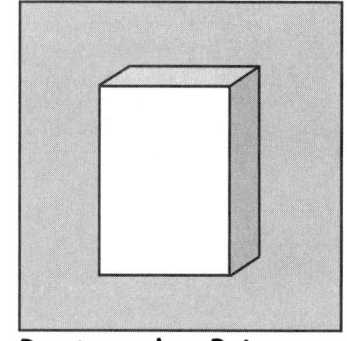

Rectangular Prism

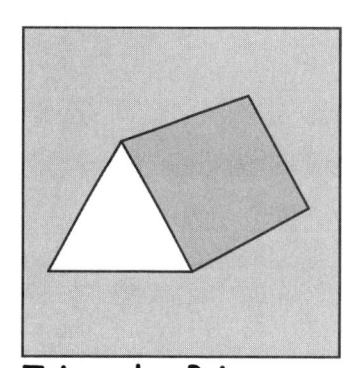

Triangular Prism

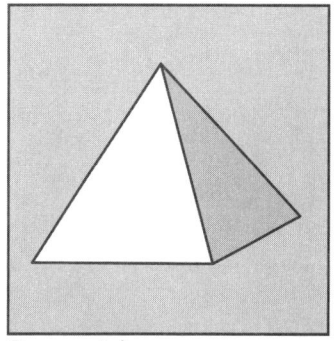

Pyramid

Cylinder

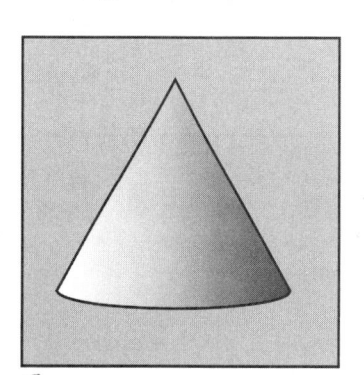

Cone

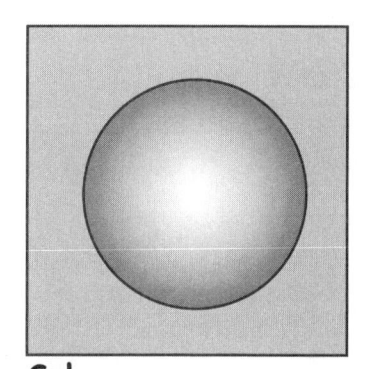

Sphere

Examples of Object Movement

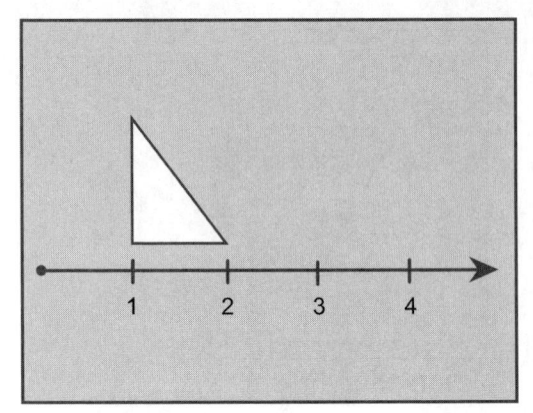

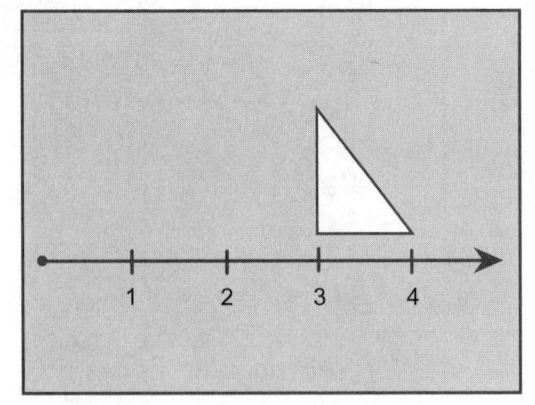

Translation or Slide

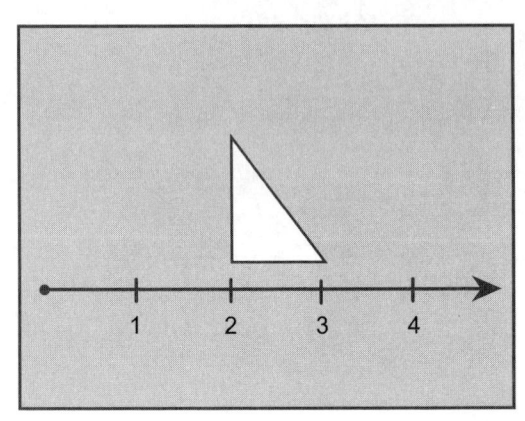

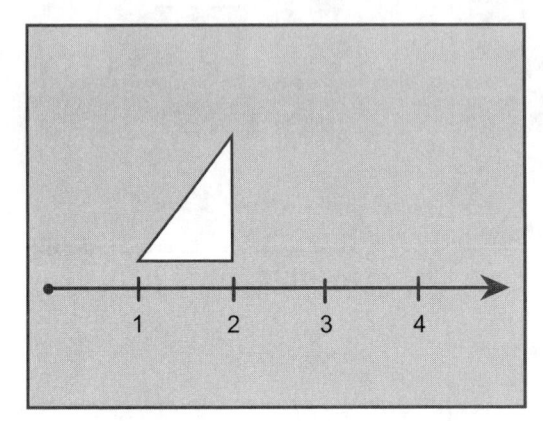

Reflection or Flip

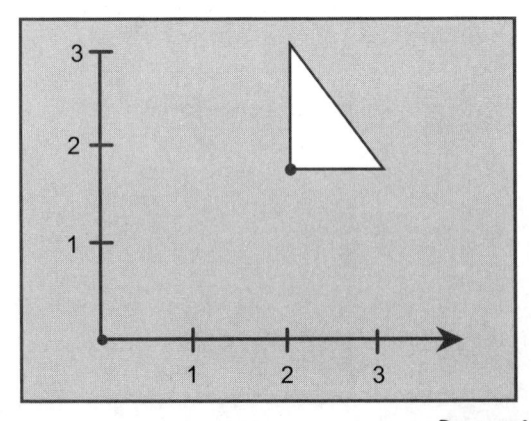

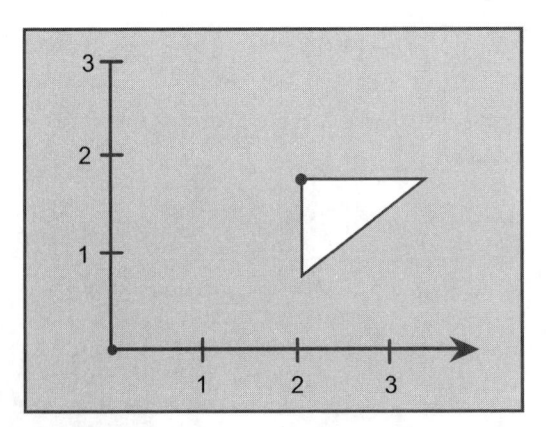

Rotation or Turn

Mathematics Practice Test 1

Mathematics **M**

Directions:

Today you will be taking a practice Mathematics assessment. This is a test of how well you understand mathematics. The test consists of questions about numbers, measurement, shapes, graphs, and patterns. Two different types of questions appear on this test: multiple choice and constructed response.

There are several important things to remember:

1. Read each question carefully. Think about what is being asked. If a graph or other diagram goes with the question, look at it carefully to help you answer the question. Then choose or write the answer that you think is best.

2. When you write your answers, write them neatly and clearly in the space provided using a pencil.

3. When you answer a multiple choice question, make sure you fill in the circle next to the answer. Mark only one answer.

4. If you do not know the answer to a question, skip it and go on. If you have time, go back to the questions you skipped and answer them before you hand in your Student Workbook.

5. If you finish the test early, you may check over your work. When you are finished and your Student Workbook has been collected, you may take out your silent work.

Mathematics

Use Pencil Please

1. How is the number 900,300 written in words?

   ○ A. nine hundred three

   ○ B. nine thousand three hundred

   ○ C. nine hundred thousand three hundred

2. Julio, Greta, Howard, and Kendra each have a baseball card collection. Julio has 1,324 baseball cards. Greta has 1,039 baseball cards. Howard has 1,298 baseball cards. Kendra has 1,331 baseball cards.

   Who has the greatest number of baseball cards?

   ○ A. Julio

   ○ B. Howard

   ○ C. Kendra

3. Fillippe wants to buy his brother a balloon. The balloon costs 80¢. He has 4 quarters and 4 dimes.

   Which group of coins would be enough to pay for the balloon?

   ○ A. (3 quarters)

   ○ B. (1 quarter, 4 dimes)

   ○ C. (2 quarters, 3 dimes)

Mathematics

4. What fraction of the flowers below has petals that are shaded?

_____

Show how you found your answer using pictures, words or numbers.

5. Pat collected 16 arrowheads before he went camping. After he went camping, he had 26 arrowheads in all.

   Which number sentence could be used to find how many arrowheads Pat found on his camping trip?

   ○ A. ☐ − 26 = 16

   ○ B. ☐ − 16 = 26

   ○ C. 16 + ☐ = 26

Mathematics   **Use Pencil Please**

6. Rob had 12 seeds and 3 pots to put them into. He put the same number of seeds into each pot.

Write a number sentence to show how to find the number of seeds he put into each pot.

Go to next page

7. Mrs. Garcia has 3 cupcake pans. Each pan has room for 9 cupcakes.

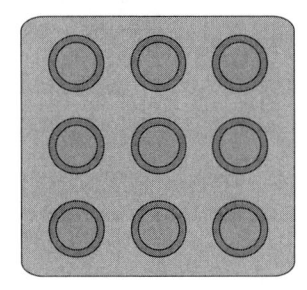

How many cupcakes can Mrs. Garcia bake at one time?

○ A. 18 cupcakes

○ B. 24 cupcakes

○ C. 27 cupcakes

Mathematics

8. The wallpaper in Lisa's room has lions on it. On one wall, Lisa counted 39 lions.

   About how many lions are on that wall?

   ○ A. 30
   ○ B. 35
   ○ C. 40

9. Maria bought 18 oranges at the market. Juan bought 29 oranges.

   About how many more oranges did Juan buy than Maria?

   ○ A. 10 oranges
   ○ B. 20 oranges
   ○ C. 30 oranges

Go to next page

10. Guadalupe is making punch for a party. For each pitcher of punch she makes, she uses 2 cans of soda and 1 container of orange juice.

Which of the following shows how many cans of soda and containers of orange juice Guadalupe will need to make 3 pitchers of punch?

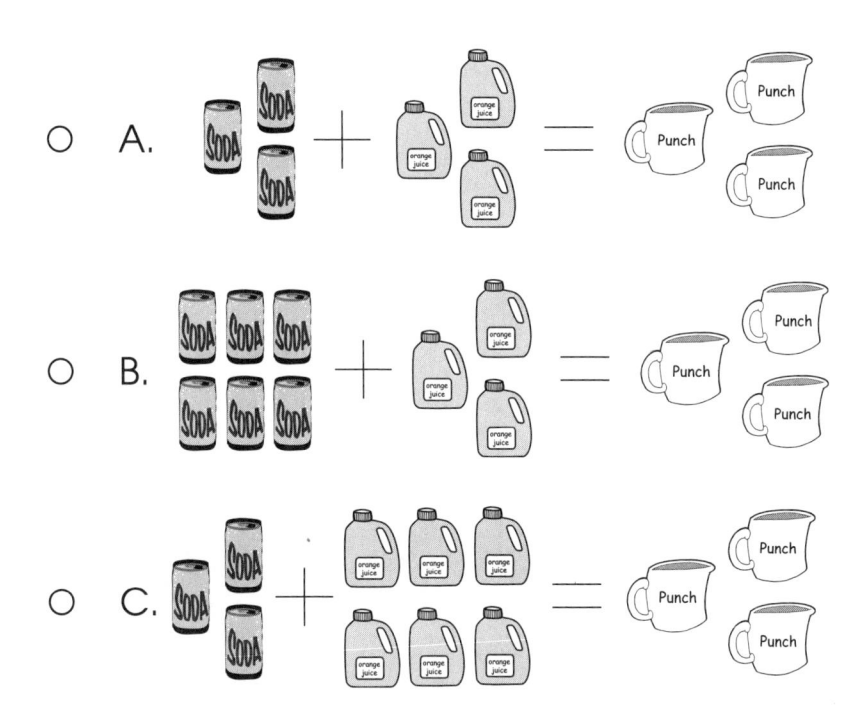

○ A.

○ B.

○ C.

Go to next page

Mathematics

11. Tim bought 6 small cans of soda. He read that each can contains 8 ounces of soda. He made a chart showing the number of ounces found in 5 of his cans.

Cans	Ounces
1	8
2	16
3	24
4	32
5	40
6	

How many ounces are in 6 cans of soda?

○ A. 48 ounces

○ B. 50 ounces

○ C. 58 ounces

12. There are 3 wheels on a tricycle.

Which of the charts below shows this information?

○ A.

Tricycles	Wheels
3	3
6	6
9	9

○ B.

Tricycles	Wheels
1	3
3	9
6	18

○ C.

Tricycles	Wheels
3	9
6	12
9	15

13. The chart below shows information about Mrs. Stanton's flower garden. Each row has the same number of flowers.

Rows	2	3	4	5	6
Flowers	16	24	32		48

Write a number sentence that describes the pattern in the table.

_____

Find the total number of flowers planted in 5 rows.

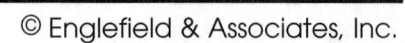

14. Which unit should be used to measure the length of a nail?

   ○ A. inch
   ○ B. foot
   ○ C. yard

15. What time is shown on the clock below?

   ○ A. 8:15
   ○ B. 8:45
   ○ C. 9:45

Mathematics

16. What temperature does the thermometer show?

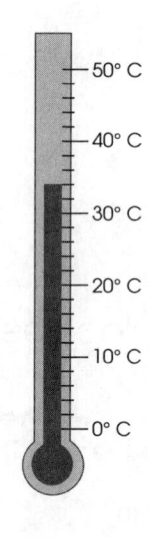

○ A. 32° C

○ B. 34° C

○ C. 36° C

17. A wall of a house is built with equal-sized bricks. Each brick is about 2 inches wide and 6 inches long.

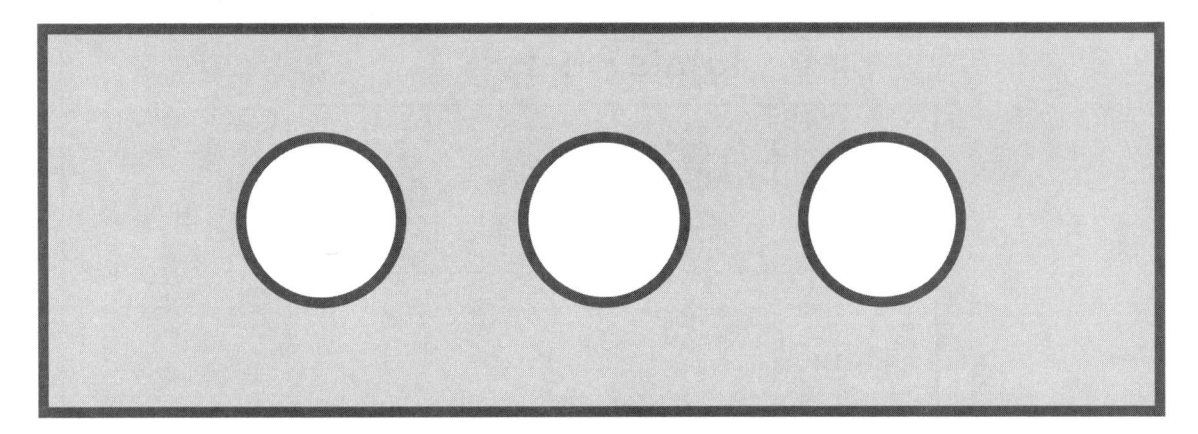

If 8 bricks are placed in a row, lengthwise, so that they are lying like the brick shown, what will be the total length of the row of bricks?

_____

Show how you found your answer using pictures, words or numbers.

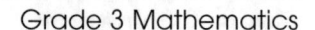

Mathematics

18. Rita has plants in 3 rooms of her house. The graph below shows how many plants are in each room.

Rita's Plants

Living Room	🪴 🪴 🪴
Kitchen	🪴
Bedroom	🪴 🪴

Each 🪴 represents 3 plants.

How many plants does Rita have in her house?

○ A. 6 plants

○ B. 12 plants

○ C. 18 plants

19. Mrs. Rielly is planning on painting the meeting room in the Recreation Center. She asked each member to vote for a color. The number of votes each color received is shown on the bar graph below.

Recreation Center Paint Color Vote

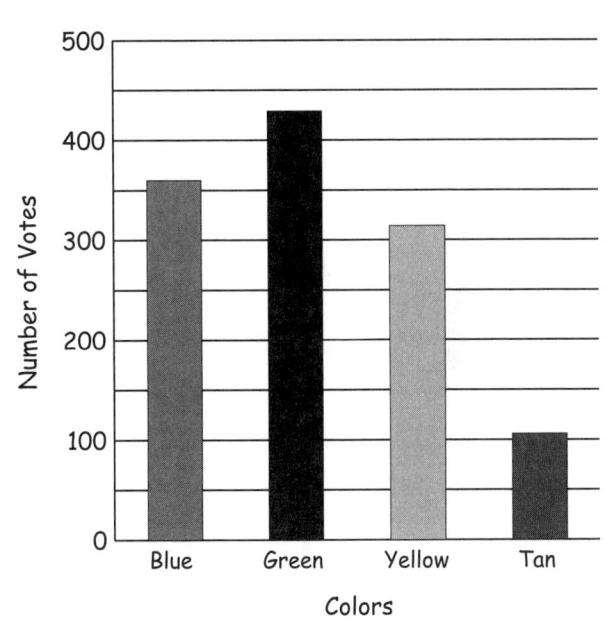

Which color will Mrs. Rielly most likely paint the meeting room?

○ A. blue

○ B. green

○ C. tan

Mathematics

20. Tara has 12 pop CDs, 4 classical CDs, 6 jazz CDs, and 10 CDs with show tunes.

    Which of the graphs below shows Tara's CD collection?

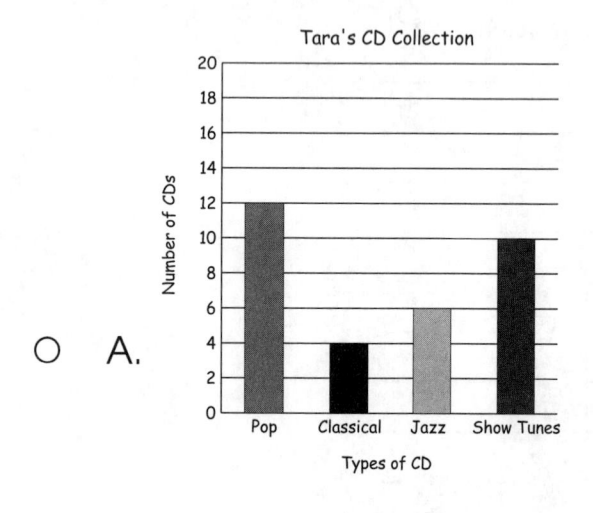

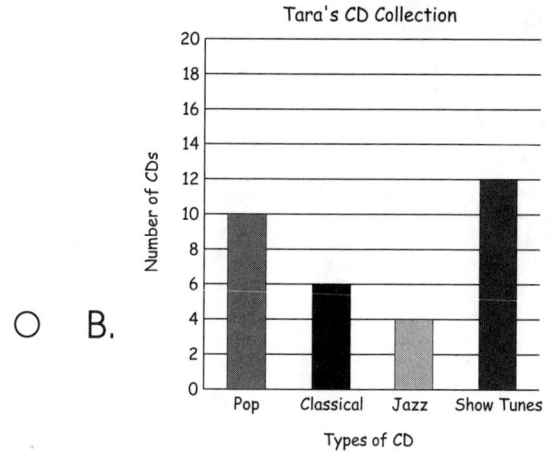

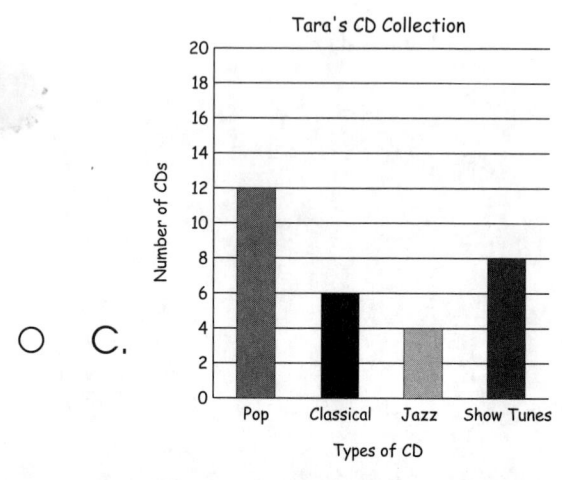

    ○ A. [Bar graph: Tara's CD Collection — Pop: 12, Classical: 4, Jazz: 6, Show Tunes: 10]

    ○ B. [Bar graph: Tara's CD Collection — Pop: 10, Classical: 6, Jazz: 4, Show Tunes: 12]

    ○ C. [Bar graph: Tara's CD Collection — Pop: 12, Classical: 6, Jazz: 4, Show Tunes: 8]

Go to next page

Show What You Know® Publishing

Grade 3 Mathematics

Practice Test 1

Mathematics M

21. In the store, Mr. Walker put out 16 books. He put an equal number of books on each of the 2 shelves.

Which picture shows how he divided the books?

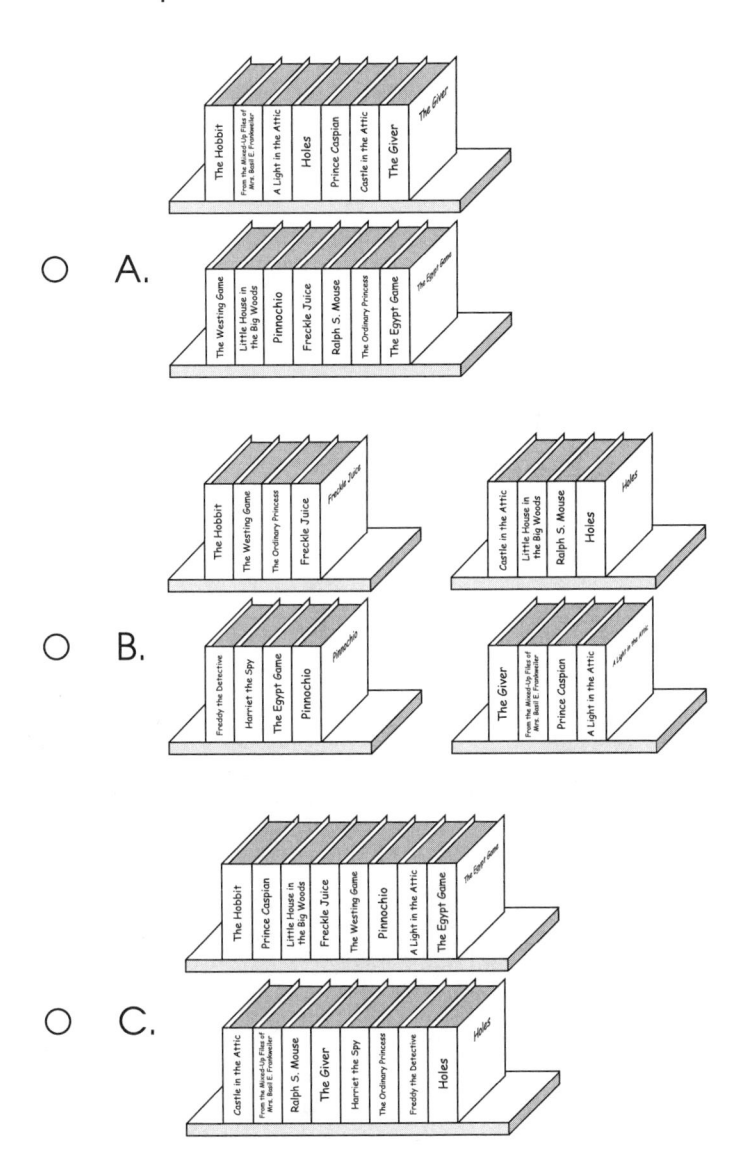

○ A.

○ B.

○ C.

Go to next page

© Englefield & Associates, Inc.   Copying is Prohibited   Student Workbook 139

Mathematics

22. What unit of measurement should be used to find the weight of a couch?

    ○ A. pounds
    ○ B. ounces
    ○ C. feet

23. Which of the following objects weighs about 30 kilograms?

    Key:
    1 gram = .002 pounds
    1 kilogram = 2.2 pounds

    ○ A. a book
    ○ B. a third grader
    ○ C. an elephant

24. Sam has a mug full of hot chocolate.

    A mug holds about

    ○ A. 1 ounce.

    ○ B. 1 cup.

    ○ C. 1 pint.

25. Which unit of measurement should be used to find the weight of a TV?

    ○ A. pounds

    ○ B. gallons

    ○ C. tons

26. Which of the following figures has the least number of sides?

    ○ A. square

    ○ B. triangle

    ○ C. pentagon

Mathematics

27. Which picture shows a line of symmetry?

○ A.

○ B.

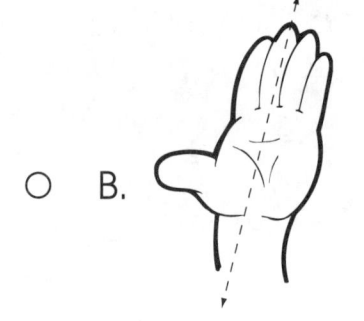

○ C.

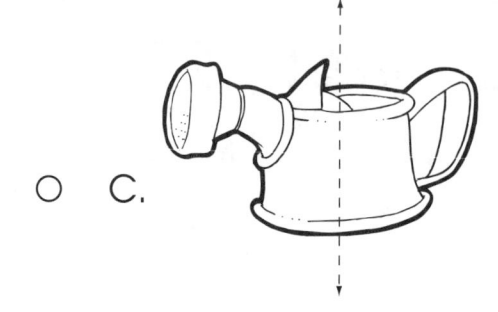

28. Which figure does NOT show a line of symmetry?

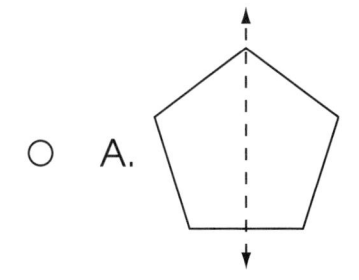

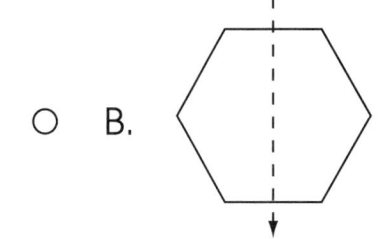

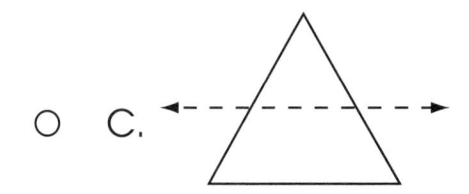

○ A.

○ B.

○ C.

Mathematics

29. Betty baked a cherry pie. She cut the pie into 8 equal pieces. Then, she and her friend Amos each ate 1 piece of pie.

Write the fraction that relates to the portion of the pie that is left.

_____

Draw a picture that shows the portion of the pie that remains after Betty and Amos each eat their part of pie.

Oliva ate 1 piece of pie.

Draw a picture that shows the portion of the pie that remains after Betty, Amos, and Oliva each eat their part of pie.

Mathematics

30. Kip has 9 video games. For every 1 video game that Kip has, his brother has 3 video games.

    Which of the number sentences below represents the number of video games Kip's brother has?

    ○ A. 9 + 3 = ☐

    ○ B. 9 x 3 = ☐

    ○ C. 9 ÷ 3 = ☐

31. Glenn plays tennis every Saturday. On the first Saturday, he played for 30 minutes. On the second Saturday, he played for 50 minutes. On the third Saturday, he played for 70 minutes.

    If the pattern continues, for how long would he most likely play on the fourth Saturday?

    ○ A. 80 minutes

    ○ B. 90 minutes

    ○ C. 100 minutes

Go to next page

32. Holly read 3 books in September. She read 6 books in October. She read 9 books in November.

    If the pattern continues, how many books will Holly most likely read in December?

    ○ A. 9

    ○ B. 12

    ○ C. 27

33. Nathan had 12 books. He gave his sister 6 books. Then, his mother gave him 4 new books.

    What number sentence could be used to find how many books Nathan has now?

    ○ A. 12 − 6 + 4 = ☐

    ○ B. 12 + 6 − 4 = ☐

    ○ C. 12 + 6 + 4 = ☐

Mathematics Use Pencil Please

34. Carmen has four cats. Jove weighs 14 pounds. Tate weighs 12 pounds. Whiskers weighs 10 pounds, and Lily weighs 18 pounds. Carmen weighs 100 pounds more than the total weight of the cats.

    How many pounds does Carmen weigh?

    ○ A. 54 pounds
    ○ B. 146 pounds
    ○ C. 154 pounds

35. Yoshi was selling shirts at the fair. He had 2,781 shirts to sell. The total number of shirts sold was between 2,000 and 2,400.

    What is a reasonable number of shirts that Yoshi would have left over at the end of the fair?

    ○ A. 200 shirts
    ○ B. 400 shirts
    ○ C. 900 shirts

Go to next page

36. The chart below shows the price list for snacks at the zoo.

Snack	Cost
Popcorn	$1.00
French Fries	$3.00
Onion Rings	$4.00
Soda	$2.00

Keith has $5.00 and wants to buy 2 snacks.

List two snacks Keith can buy and still have money left over.

_____

_____

How much money will Keith have left over after he buys his snacks?

Mathematics

Can Keith buy 3 items from the menu? _____

Show or explain why or why not.

37. On the grid below, which point is located at the coordinates (1, 5)?

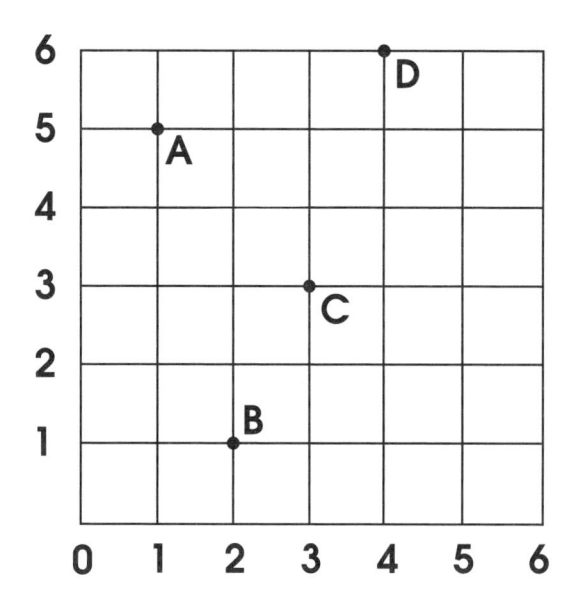

- A. point A
- B. point B
- C. point C

38. The shoe sizes of the five members of Yolanda's family are 4, 6, 6, 8, and 9.

What is the mode of the shoe sizes in Yolanda's family?

- A. 5
- B. 6
- C. 7

Mathematics

Use Pencil Please

39. The students in Mr. Sefton's class took a survey to see what holiday was most popular with the students in their class. They put their results into the bar graph below.

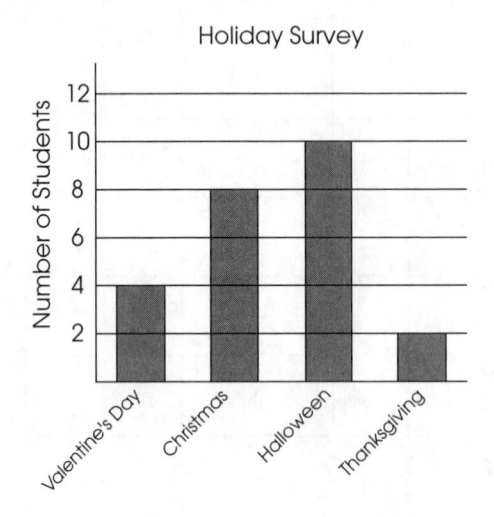

Holiday Survey

(Bar graph showing Number of Students for each holiday: Valentine's Day = 4, Christmas = 8, Halloween = 10, Thanksgiving = 2)

What is the total number of students in Mr. Sefton's class.

_____

Show how you found your answer using pictures, words or numbers.

Go to next page

40. Look at the shape below.

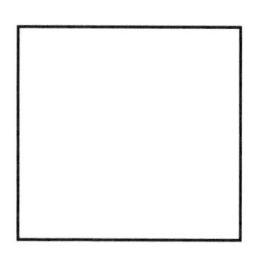

What shape is shown?

_____

Name two properties that define this shape.

Mathematics Practice Test 2

Mathematics **M**

Directions:

Today you will be taking a practice Mathematics assessment. This is a test of how well you understand mathematics. The test consists of questions about numbers, measurement, shapes, graphs, and patterns. Two different types of questions appear on this test: multiple choice and constructed response.

There are several important things to remember:

1. Read each question carefully. Think about what is being asked. If a graph or other diagram goes with the question, look at it carefully to help you answer the question. Then choose or write the answer that you think is best.

2. When you write your answers, write them neatly and clearly in the space provided using a pencil.

3. When you answer a multiple choice question, make sure you fill in the circle next to the answer. Mark only one answer.

4. If you do not know the answer to a question, skip it and go on. If you have time, go back to the questions you skipped and answer them before you hand in your Student Workbook.

5. If you finish the test early, you may check over your work. When you are finished and your Student Workbook has been collected, you may take out your silent work.

Go to next page

Mathematics

1. Which figure has $\frac{5}{6}$ shaded?

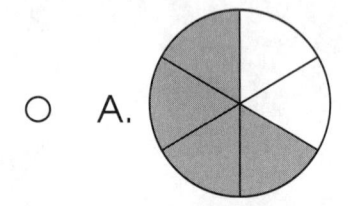

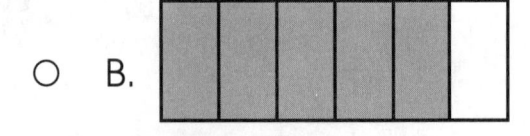

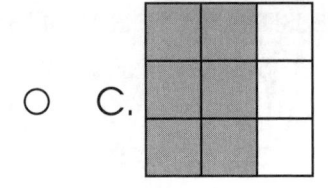

   ○ A.

   ○ B.

   ○ C.

2. Lindsay had 72¢. After she bought an apple, she had 19¢ left. How much did the apple cost?

   ○ A. 53¢

   ○ B. 63¢

   ○ C. 91¢

3. Solve the following problem.

$$\begin{array}{r} 703 \\ + 698 \\ \hline \end{array}$$

- ○ A. 1,391
- ○ B. 1,401
- ○ C. 1,491

Mathematics

4. Cheryl had 30 dimes. She divided them into piles with 5 dimes in each pile.

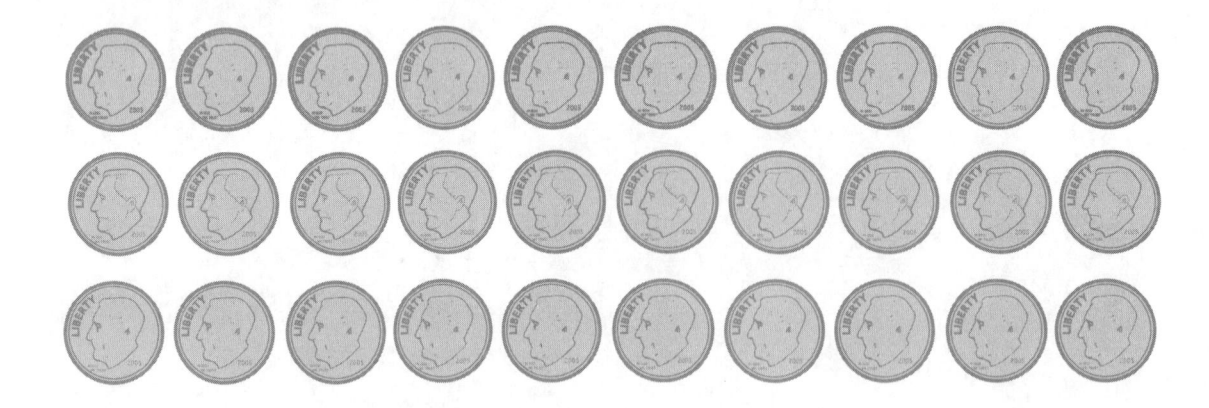

How many piles were there?

_____

Show how you found your answer using pictures, words or numbers.

5. Kathy has two packs of gum with five pieces in each pack. She wants to share the gum equally with her friends, Stephanie and Missy.

How many pieces of gum will each of the girls have if they are only given whole pieces of gum?

_____

How many whole pieces of gum are left?

_____

Show how you found your answer using pictures, words or numbers.

Mathematics

6. Look at the digital clock.

   Which clock matches the time shown on the digital clock?

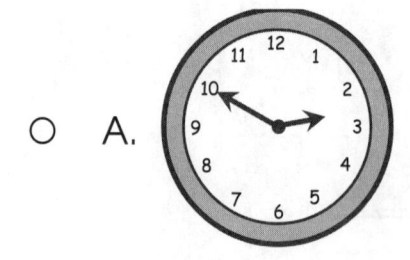

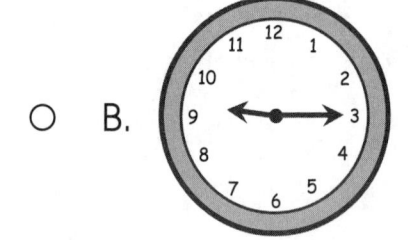

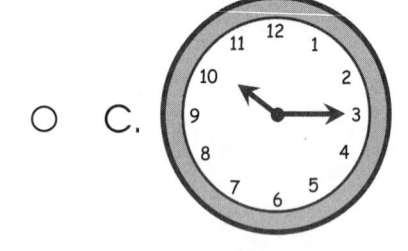

   ○ A.

   ○ B.

   ○ C.

7. Which clock shows a time between 3:00 and 4:00?

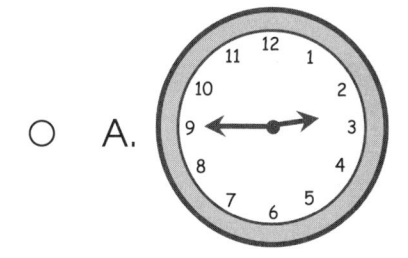

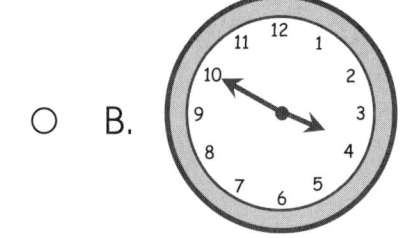

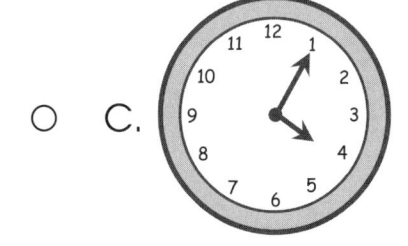

○ A.

○ B.

○ C.

Mathematics

8. Luis and Anna recorded their clarinet practice times. Each student made a tally mark for every 9 minutes of practice.

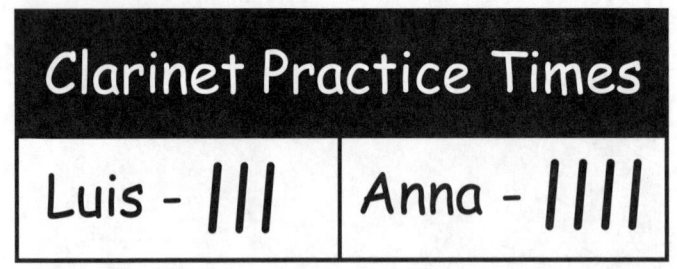

| Clarinet Practice Times ||
| Luis - ||| | Anna - |||| |

Each mark represents 9 minutes.

Which bar graph matches the information shown in the chart?

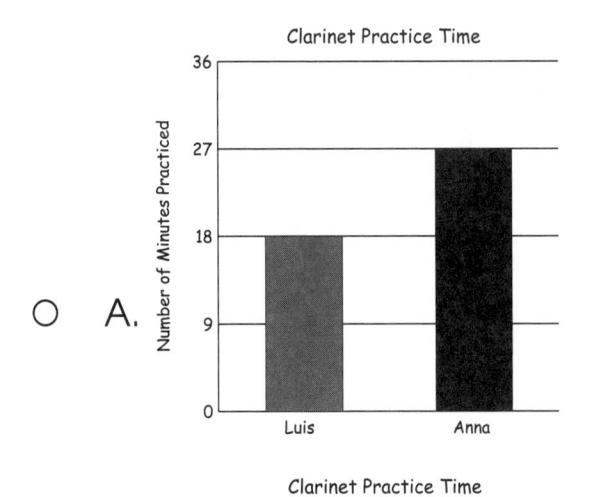

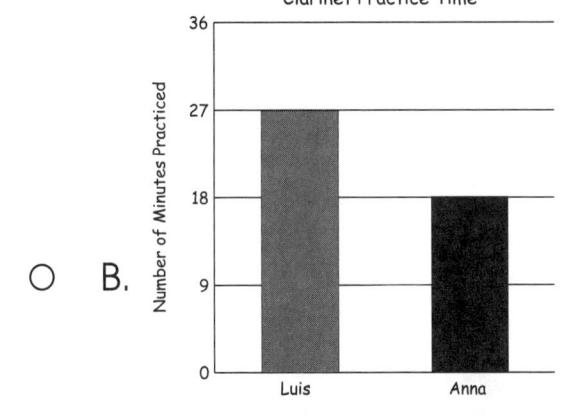

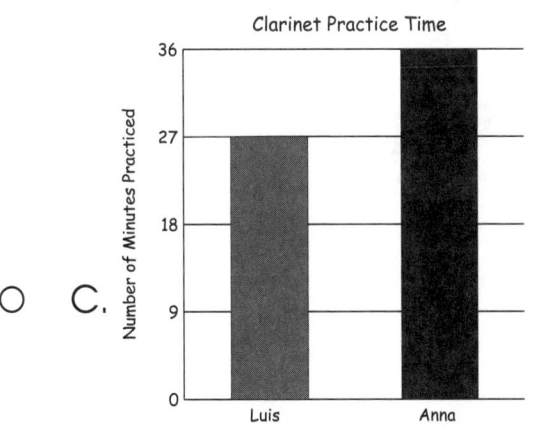

A. Clarinet Practice Time — Luis: 18, Anna: 27

B. Clarinet Practice Time — Luis: 27, Anna: 18

C. Clarinet Practice Time — Luis: 27, Anna: 36

Mathematics

9. Mr. Ying has 7 pots of tulips in his shop. Each pot has 7 flowers in it. The chart below shows how many tulips he has in 5 pots.

Pots	Tulips
1	7
2	14
3	21
4	28
5	35
6	
7	

How many tulips does he have in all 7 pots?

○ A. 51 tulips

○ B. 49 tulips

○ C. 47 tulips

10. Find the perimeter of the shape below.

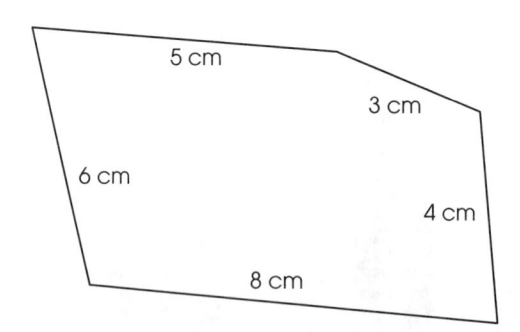

5 cm
3 cm
6 cm
4 cm
8 cm

○ A. 21 centimeters

○ B. 23 centimeters

○ C. 26 centimeters

11. Katy had 13 stuffed animals. She gave 4 of them to her cousin.

    Which number sentence could be used to find how many stuffed animals Katy has left?

    ○ A. 13 + 4 = ☐

    ○ B. 13 − 4 = ☐

    ○ C. 13 ÷ 4 = ☐

12. What is the missing number in the number pattern below?

    48, 42, 36, 30, _____, 18, 12

    ○ A. 24
    ○ B. 23
    ○ C. 22

Go to next page

Mathematics

Use Pencil Please

13. Four students in Mrs. Campbell's class won blue ribbons on Field Day. Jessica won 2 ribbons, Sun and Marcus won 4 ribbons each, and Phillip won 3 ribbons.

    Which pictograph shows this information?

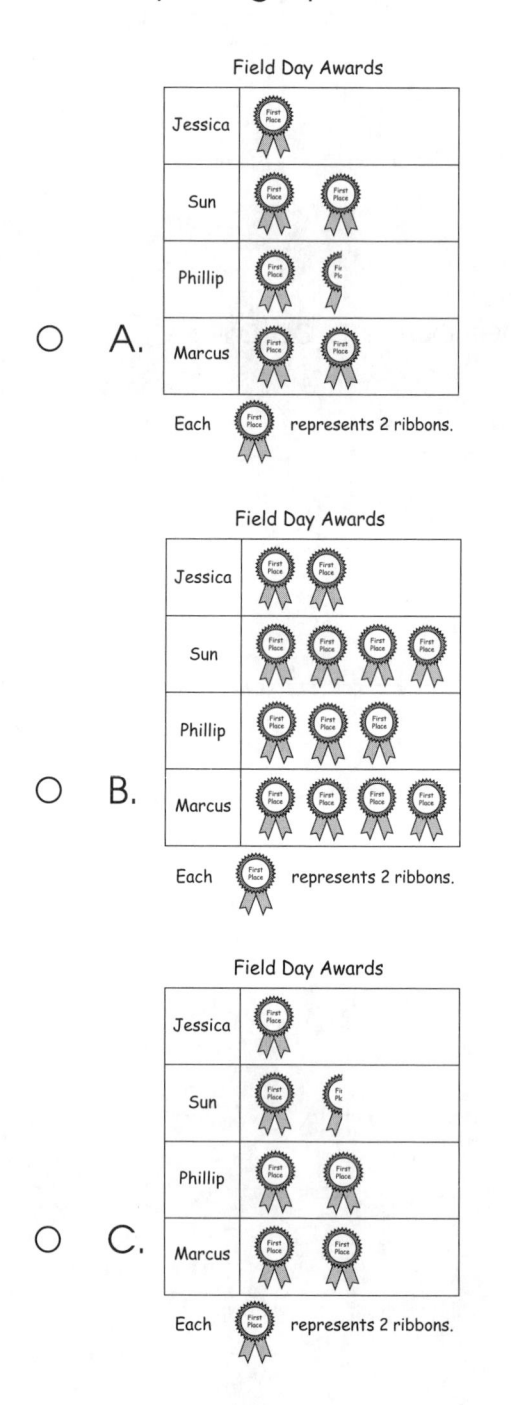

    ○ A. Field Day Awards
    | Jessica | 🎀 |
    | Sun | 🎀 🎀 |
    | Phillip | 🎀 🎀(half) |
    | Marcus | 🎀 🎀 |

    Each 🎀 represents 2 ribbons.

    ○ B. Field Day Awards
    | Jessica | 🎀 🎀 |
    | Sun | 🎀 🎀 🎀 🎀 |
    | Phillip | 🎀 🎀 🎀 |
    | Marcus | 🎀 🎀 🎀 🎀 |

    Each 🎀 represents 2 ribbons.

    ○ C. Field Day Awards
    | Jessica | 🎀 |
    | Sun | 🎀 🎀(half) |
    | Phillip | 🎀 🎀 |
    | Marcus | 🎀 🎀 |

    Each 🎀 represents 2 ribbons.

Go to next page ➡

14. Mrs. Goodrich is having a party. She needs 32 servings of lemonade. Each carton of lemonade has 10 servings in it.

    How many cartons should Mrs. Goodrich buy so that she can make 32 servings?

    ○ A. 5 cartons

    ○ B. 4 cartons

    ○ C. 3 cartons

15. The chart below shows how many apples are needed to make jars of applesauce.

Jars	1	2	3	4
Apples	8	16	24	32

    According to the pattern in the chart, how many apples would be used to make 6 jars of applesauce?

    ○ A. 40 apples

    ○ B. 48 apples

    ○ C. 56 apples

Mathematics

16. Mr. Oonagi's class took a field trip to a local berry farm. The farmer told the class that he uses the size of the berries to help him decide what they would be best used for.

Use	Berry Size
Juice	0-2 ounces
Jam	2-4 ounces
Preserves	4-5 ounces
Canning	5+ ounces

If the farmer wants to make jam and preserves, which berry size would be best for him to use?

○ A. 2 ounces

○ B. 4 ounces

○ C. 6 ounces

Go to next page

17. The thermometer shows the high temperature for today.

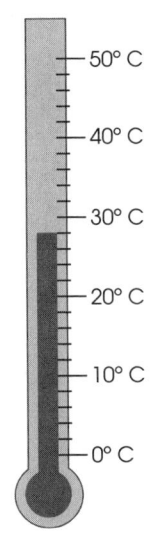

- 50° C
- 40° C
- 30° C
- 20° C
- 10° C
- 0° C

What is the temperature on the thermometer?

_____

Show how you found your answer using pictures, words or numbers.

Go to next page

Mathematics

18. Albert has a model car collection on his shelf. He keeps 14 cars on the top shelf, 6 cars on the middle shelf, and 17 cars on the bottom shelf.

    How many cars does Albert have?

    _____

    Write a number sentence Albert might use to find how many cars he has in his collection.

19. Akiko is taking piano lessons. She learns 7 short songs each month.

Months	Songs
1	7
2	
3	21

After two months, how many songs will Akiko have learned?

○ A. 7 songs

○ B. 14 songs

○ C. 21 songs

Mathematics

20. The third-grade students at Redwood Elementary School voted for their favorite ice cream flavors. The bar graph below shows the number of students who voted for each flavor.

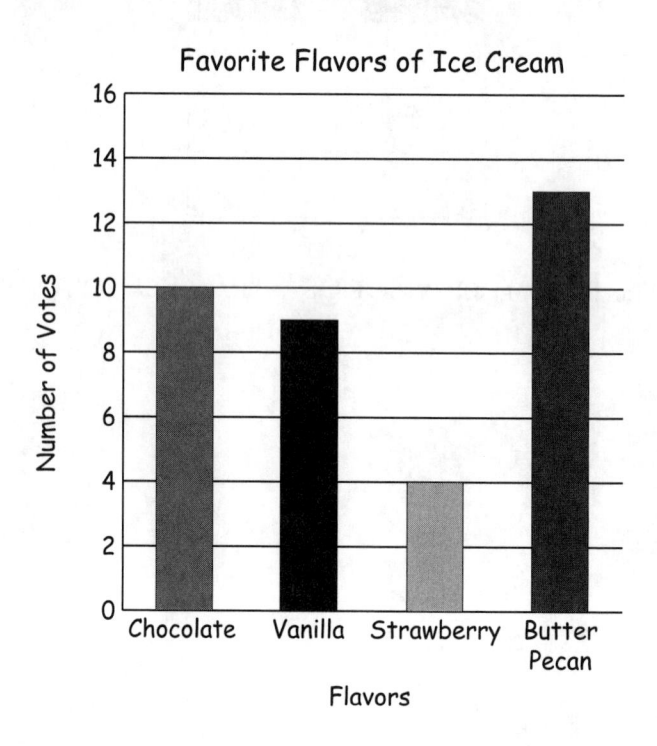

Favorite Flavors of Ice Cream

(Bar graph showing: Chocolate = 10, Vanilla = 9, Strawberry = 4, Butter Pecan = 13)

Which flavor will the teachers most likely choose to get for the year-end party?

○ A. chocolate

○ B. strawberry

○ C. butter pecan

21. These squares follow a pattern.

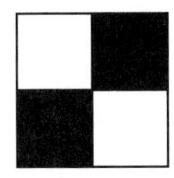

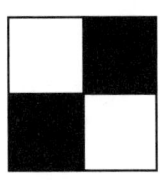

Which square will come next in the pattern?

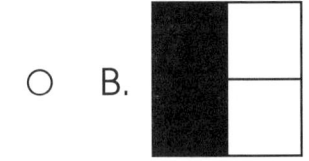

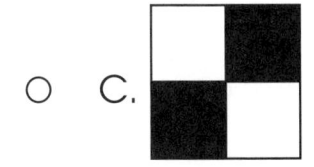

○ A.

○ B.

○ C.

22. Which figure below has a line of symmetry?

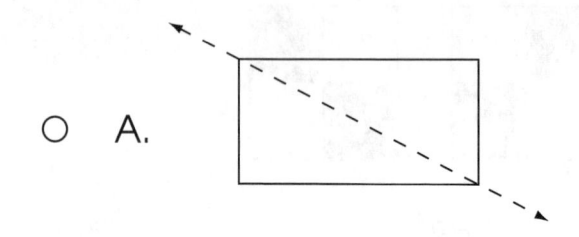

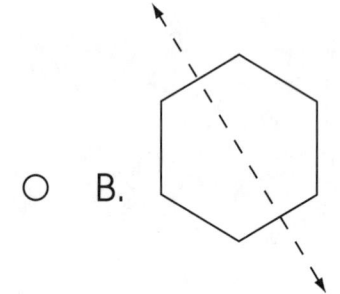

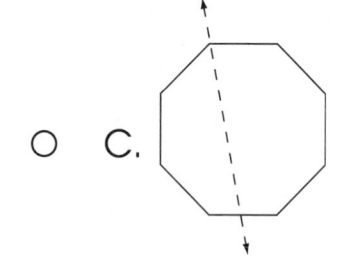

○ A.

○ B.

○ C.

23. Mr. Drake is buying potato chips for his neighborhood picnic. They come in boxes with 8 bags in each box.

What is the lowest number of boxes he can buy if he needs 50 bags of chips?

- ○ A. 6 boxes
- ○ B. 7 boxes
- ○ C. 8 boxes

24. The children in the Clark family record their heights every year on their birthdays.

Age	4	5	6	7	8	9	10
Trevor	34 in.	36 in.	38 in.	40 in.	42 in.	44 in.	46 in.
Megan	33 in.	35 in.	37 in.	39 in.	41 in.	43 in.	45 in.
Bob	36 in.	38 in.	40 in.	42 in.	44 in.	46 in.	48 in.

Using the information in the chart, which of the following is true?

- ○ A. When Bob and Megan were the same ages, Bob was never shorter than Megan.
- ○ B. When Megan and Trevor were the same ages, Megan was always taller than Trevor.
- ○ C. When Trevor and Bob were the same ages, Trevor was always taller than Bob.

Go to next page

Mathematics

25. Mrs. Holt has twin babies named Jesse and Randy. She recorded the weight of each boy two times. She used bar graphs to show how much the boys weighed in September and in March.

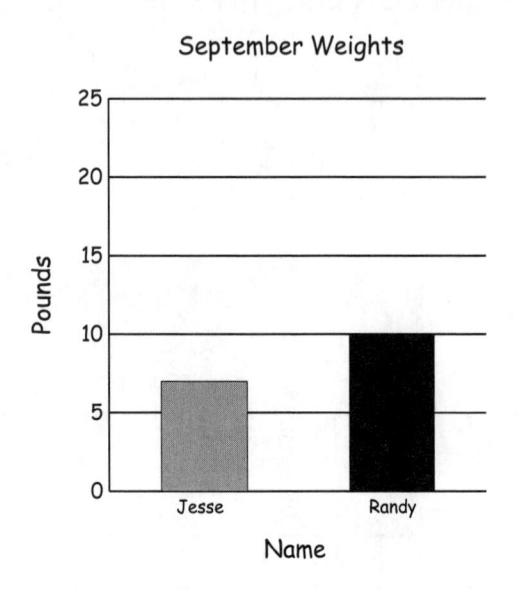

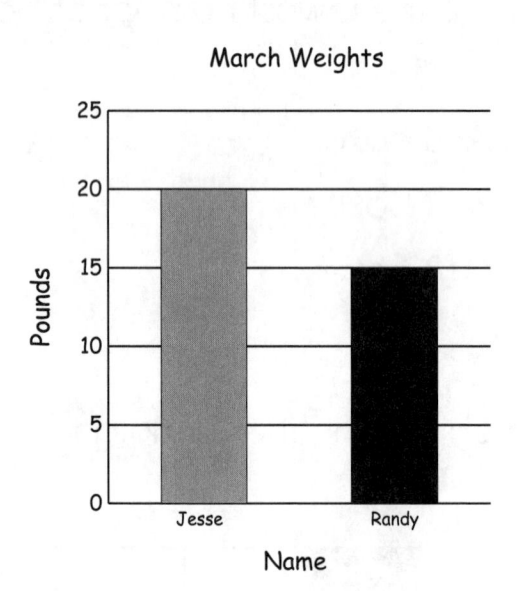

How much did Jesse weigh in March?

- A. 7 pounds
- B. 15 pounds
- C. 20 pounds

26. What number is the same as eight hundred ninety-six thousand five hundred two?

- A. 800,096,502
- B. 896,502
- C. 896,520

27. Which unit should be used to measure the height of a door?

- A. mile
- B. foot
- C. millimeter

Mathematics

28. Look at the figure below.

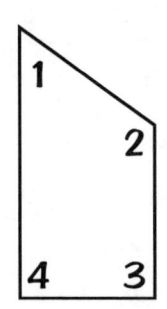

Which angle best represents an acute angle?

○ A. angle 1
○ B. angle 2
○ C. angle 3

29. A pail holds about

    ○ A. 3 ounces.

    ○ B. 3 pounds.

    ○ C. 3 gallons.

30. What unit of measurement should be used to find the capacity of a bathtub?

    ○ A. grams

    ○ B. meters

    ○ C. liters

Mathematics

31. The map below shows the route Jeremy's mom drove to take him to see his friend Eddie.

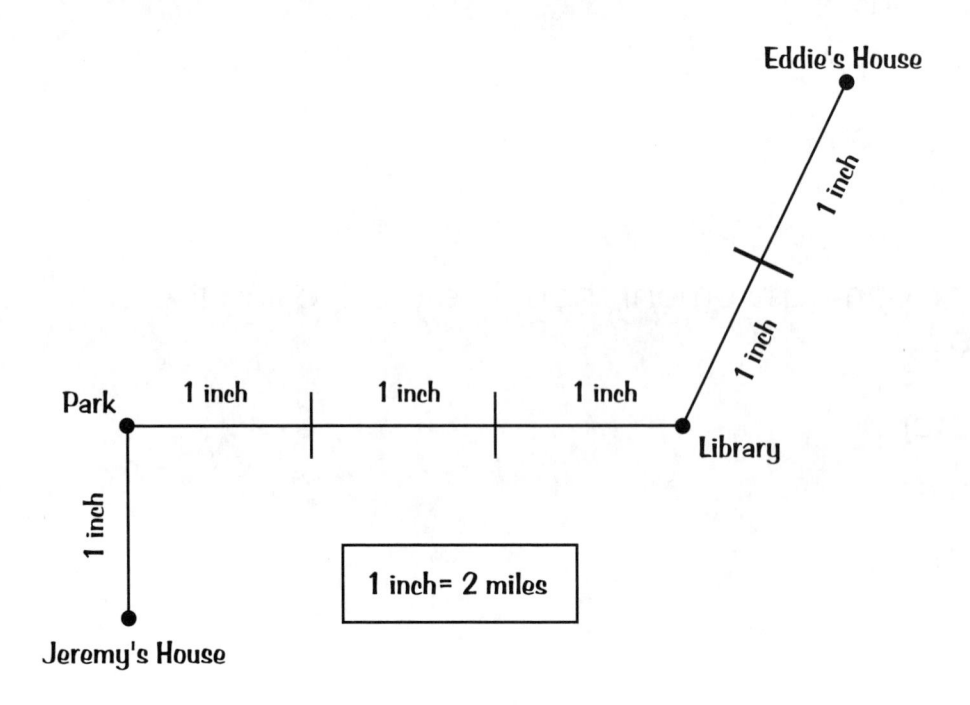

[Map showing: Jeremy's House to Park (1 inch), Park to Library (1 inch + 1 inch + 1 inch), Library to Eddie's House (1 inch + 1 inch). Scale: 1 inch = 2 miles]

What is the actual distance between the park and the library?

- A. 3 miles
- B. 6 miles
- C. 12 miles

32. Which figure does NOT have a line of symmetry?

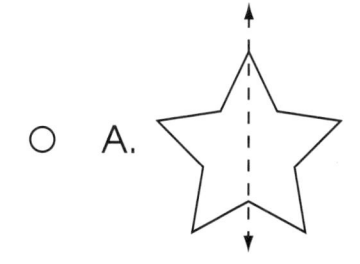

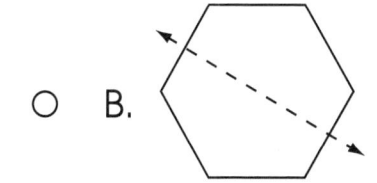

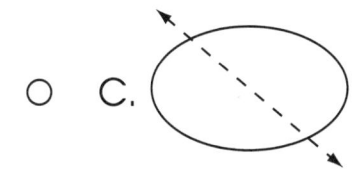

○ A.

○ B.

○ C.

Mathematics

33. Which of the following is the approximate weight of a 20-pound tire?

Key:
1 gram = .002 pounds
1 kilogram = 2.2 pounds

○ A. 90 grams

○ B. 9 kilograms

○ C. 90 kilograms

34. Which shape has the greatest number of obtuse angles?

○ A.

○ B.

○ C.

35. Nicole is 6 years old. Nicole's sister Shawna is 5 years older.

Which number sentence best represents Shawna's age?

○ A. 6 + 5 = ☐

○ B. ☐ + 5 = 6

○ C. 6 x 5 = ☐

Mathematics

36. Ann earned $5.00 washing the dog. She spent $3.50 on a comic book and $0.50 on a candy bar.

    How much money does Ann have after she makes her purchases?

    _____

    Show how you found your answer using pictures, words or numbers.

Ann found $0.73 on the way home.

How much money does Ann have when she gets home?

Mathematics

37. Look at the square below.

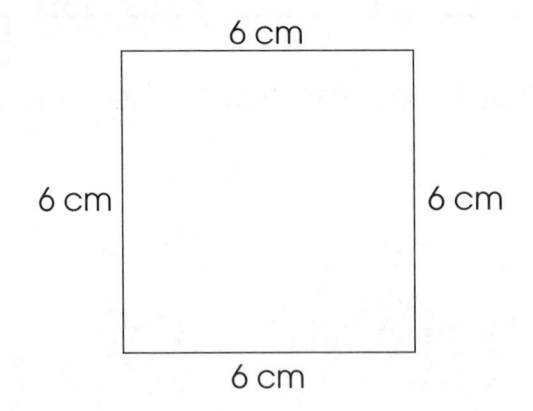

```
        6 cm
    ┌─────────┐
    │         │
6 cm│         │6 cm
    │         │
    └─────────┘
        6 cm
```

What is the perimeter of the square?

_____

How much larger is the perimeter than the length of one side of the square?

_____

_____

_____

_____

Go to next page

38. A coordinate grid is shown below.

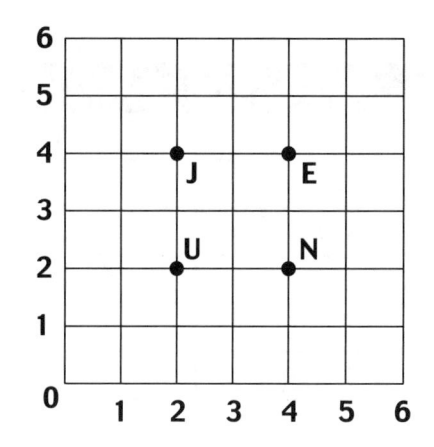

What are the coordinates of point N on the grid?

○ A. (2, 2)

○ B. (4, 4)

○ C. (4, 2)

Mathematics

39. Mario and his friends were catching lightning bugs and putting them in jars.

Name	Bugs Caught
Mario	4
Percy	2
Quentin	5
Evelyn	3
Mary	3
Eleanor	6

What is the mode of the number of lightning bugs caught.

_____

Show how you found your answer using pictures, words or numbers.

40. Look at the shape below.

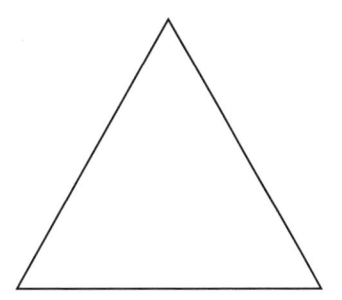

What shape is shown?
_____

Then name two properties that define this shape.

_____

_____

_____

Notes

Notes

Notes

Notes

Show What You Know on the OAA for Grade 3, Additional Products

Flash Cards for Reading and Mathematics

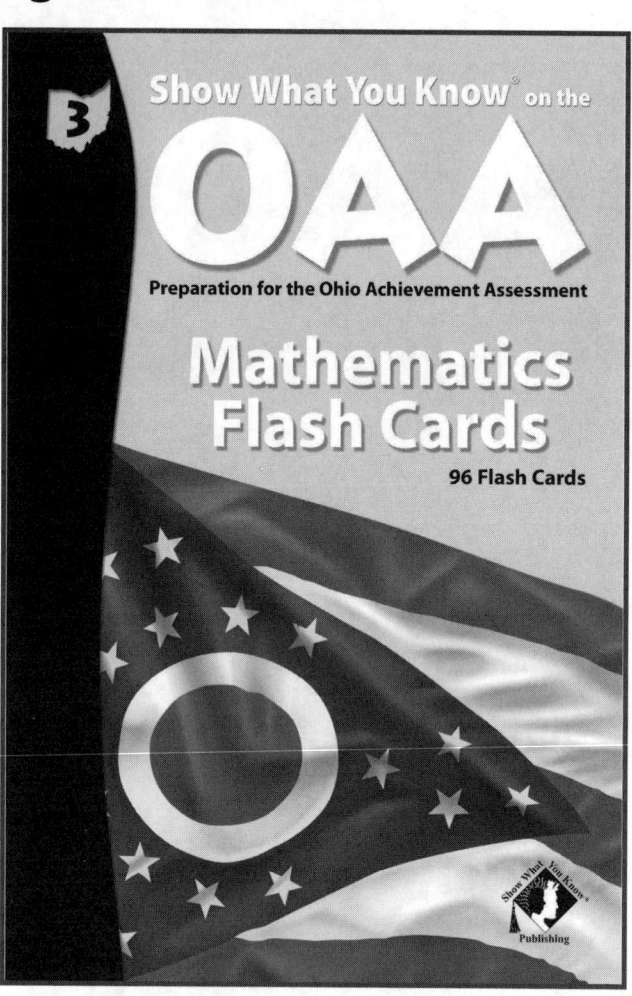

For more information, call our toll-free number: 1.877.PASSING (727-7464)
or visit our website: www.passtheoaa.com